S0-AXW-394

Jackie Joyner-Kersee

GREAT ACHIEVERS

LIVES OF THE PHYSICALLY CHALLENGED

Jackie Joyner-Kersee

CHAMPION ATHLETE

Geri Harrington

Chelsea House Publishers

New York • Philadelphia

CHELSEA HOUSE PUBLISHERS

EDITORIAL DIRECTOR   Richard Rennert
EXECUTIVE MANAGING EDITOR   Karyn Gullen Browne
COPY CHIEF   Robin James
PICTURE EDITOR   Adrian G. Allen
CREATIVE DIRECTOR   Robert Mitchell
ART DIRECTOR   Joan Ferrigno
PRODUCTION MANAGER   Sallye Scott

GREAT ACHIEVERS: LIVES OF THE PHYSICALLY CHALLENGED

SENIOR EDITOR   Kathy Kuhtz Campbell
SERIES DESIGN   Basia Niemczyc

Staff for **JACKIE JOYNER-KERSEE**

EDITORIAL ASSISTANT   Scott D. Briggs
PICTURE RESEARCHER   Ellen Dudley
COVER ILLUSTRATION   Kye Carbone

Copyright © 1995 by Chelsea House Publishers, a division of Main Line Book Co.
All rights reserved. Printed and bound in the United States of America.

First Printing

1 3 5 7 9 8 6 4 2

Library of Congress Cataloging-in-Publication Data

Harrington, Geri.
Jackie Joyner-Kersee: champion athlete / Geri Harrington.
p. cm.—(Great achievers)
Includes bibliographical references and index.
ISBN 0-7910-2085-1.
1. Joyner-Kersee, Jacqueline, 1962——Juvenile literature. 2. Track and field athletes—United States—Biography—Juvenile literature. 3. Olympics— Juvenile literature. I. Title. II. Series: Great achievers (Chelsea House Publishers)
GV697.J69H37 1995   94-38230
796.42'092—dc20   CIP
[B]   AC

FRONTISPIECE:

On August 3, 1992, Jackie Joyner-Kersee raises her arms in victory after being awarded the gold medal in the heptathlon at the Olympic Games in Barcelona, Spain.

CONTENTS

A Message for Everyone *Jerry Lewis*   7

On Facing Challenges *John Callahan*   10

1 WILLING TO WIN   13

2 THE EARLY YEARS   25

3 A GLIMPSE OF GLORY   37

4 A WHOLE NEW WORLD   49

5 GREAT EXPECTATIONS   59

6 THE DREAM COMES TRUE—ALMOST   69

7 THE BEST OF TIMES   79

8 AS GOOD AS IT GETS   91

Further Reading   105

Chronology   106

Index   110

GREAT ACHIEVERS

LIVES OF THE PHYSICALLY CHALLENGED

JIM ABBOTT
baseball star

LUDWIG VAN BEETHOVEN
composer

LOUIS BRAILLE
inventor

CHRIS BURKE
actor

JULIUS CAESAR
Roman emperor

ROY CAMPANELLA
baseball star

RAY CHARLES
musician

ROBERT DOLE
politician

STEPHEN HAWKING
physicist

JACKIE JOYNER-KERSEE
champion athlete

HELEN KELLER
humanitarian

RON KOVIC
antiwar activist

MARIO LEMIEUX
ice hockey star

MARLEE MATLIN
actress

JOHN MILTON
poet

MARY TYLER MOORE
actress

FLANNERY O'CONNOR
author

ITZHAK PERLMAN
violinist

FRANKLIN D. ROOSEVELT
U.S. president

HENRI DE TOULOUSE-LAUTREC
artist

STEVIE WONDER
musician

A Message for Everyone

Jerry Lewis

Just 44 years ago—when I was the ripe old age of 23—an incredible stroke of fate rocketed me to overnight stardom as an entertainer. After the initial shock wore off, I began to have a very strong feeling that, in return for all life had given me, I must find a way of giving something back. At just that moment, a deeply moving experience in my personal life persuaded me to take up the leadership of a fledgling battle to defeat a then little-known group of diseases called muscular dystrophy, as well as other related neuromuscular diseases—all of which are disabling and, in the worst cases, cut life short.

In 1950, when the Muscular Dystrophy Association (MDA)—of which I am national chairman—was established, physical disability was looked on as a matter of shame. Franklin Roosevelt, who guided America through World War II from a wheelchair, and Harold Russell, the World War II hero who lost both hands in battle, then became an Academy Award–winning movie star and chairman of the President's Committee on Employment of the Handicapped, were the exceptions. One of the reasons that muscular dystrophy and related diseases were so little known was that people who had been disabled by them were hidden at home, away from the pity and discomfort with which they were generally regarded by society. As I got to know and began working with people who have disabilities, I quickly learned what a tragic mistake this perception was. And my determination to correct this terrible problem soon became as great as my commitment to see disabling neuromuscular diseases wiped from the face of the earth.

I have long wondered why it never occurs to us, as we experience the knee-jerk inclination to feel sorry for people who are physically disabled, that lives such as those led by President Roosevelt, Harold Russell, and all of the extraordinary people profiled in this Great Achievers series demonstrate unmistakably how wrong we are. Physical disability need not be something that blights life and destroys opportunity for personal fulfillment and accomplishment. On the contrary, as people such as Ray Charles, Stephen Hawking, and Ron Kovic prove, physical disability can be a spur to greatness rather than a condemnation of emptiness.

In fact, if my experience with physically disabled people can be taken as a guide, as far as accomplishment is concerned, they have a slight edge on the rest of us. The unusual challenges they face require finding greater-than-average sources of energy and determination to achieve much of what able-bodied people take for granted. Often, this ultimately translates into a lifetime of superior performance in whatever endeavor people with disabilities choose to pursue.

If you have watched my Labor Day Telethon over the years, you know exactly what I am talking about. Annually, we introduce to tens of millions of Americans people whose accomplishments would distinguish them regardless of their physical conditions—top-ranking executives, physicians, scientists, lawyers, musicians, and artists. The message I hope the audience receives is not that these extraordinary individuals have achieved what they have by overcoming a dreadful disadvantage that the rest of us are lucky not to have to endure. Rather, I hope our viewers reflect on the fact that these outstanding people have been ennobled and strengthened by the tremendous challenges they have faced.

In 1992, MDA, which has grown over the past four decades into one of the world's leading voluntary health agencies, established a personal achievement awards program to demonstrate to the nation that the distinctive qualities of people with disabilities are by no means confined to the famous. What could have been more appropriate or timely in that year of the implementation of the 1990 Americans with Disabilities Act than to take an action that could perhaps finally achieve the alteration of public perception of disability, which MDA had struggled over four decades to achieve?

On Labor Day, 1992, it was my privilege to introduce to America MDA's inaugural national personal achievement award winner, Steve Mikita, assistant attorney general of the state of Utah. Steve graduated magna cum laude from Duke University as its first wheelchair student in history and was subsequently named the outstanding young lawyer of the year by the Utah Bar Association. After he spoke on the Telethon with an eloquence that caused phones to light up from coast to coast, people asked me where he had been all this time and why they had not known of him before, so deeply impressed were they by him. I answered that he and thousands like him have been here all along. We just have not adequately *noticed* them.

It is my fervent hope that we can eliminate indifference once and for all and make it possible for all of our fellow citizens with disabilities to gain their rightfully high place in our society.

ON FACING CHALLENGES

John Callahan

I was paralyzed for life in 1972, at the age of 21. A friend and I were driving in a Volkswagen on a hot July night, when he smashed the car at full speed into a utility pole. He suffered only minor injuries. But my spinal cord was severed during the crash, leaving me without any feeling from my diaphragm downward. The only muscles I could move were some in my upper body and arms, and I could also extend my fingers. After spending a lot of time in physical therapy, it became possible for me to grasp a pen.

I've always loved to draw. When I was a kid, I made pictures of everything from Daffy Duck (one of my lifelong role models) to caricatures of my teachers and friends. I've always been a people watcher, it seems; and I've always looked at the world in a sort of skewed way. Everything I see just happens to translate immediately into humor. And so, humor has become my way of coping. As the years have gone by, I have developed a tremendous drive to express my humor by drawing cartoons.

The key to cartooning is to put a different spin on the expected, the normal. And that's one reason why many of my cartoons deal with the disabled: amputees, quadriplegics, paraplegics, the blind. The public is not used to seeing them in cartoons.

But there's another reason why my subjects are often disabled men and women. I'm sick and tired of people who presume to speak for the disabled. Call me a cripple, call me a gimp, call me paralyzed for life.

Just don't call me something I'm not. I'm not "differently abled," and my cartoons show that disabled people should not be treated any differently than anyone else.

All of the men, women, and children who are profiled in the Great Achievers series share this in common: their various handicaps have not prevented them from accomplishing great things. Their life stories are worth knowing about because they have found the strength and courage to develop their talents and to follow their dreams as fully as they can.

Whether able-bodied or disabled, a person must strive to overcome obstacles. There's nothing greater than to see a person who faces challenges and conquers them, regardless of his or her limitations.

On July 28, 1984, atop a moving stairway, Rafer Johnson, the 1960 decathlon gold medalist, lights the Olympic rings with the Olympic Torch at the Los Angeles Coliseum for the opening of the 23rd Olympic Games. Jackie Joyner competed in these Olympics, her first, at the age of 22.

1

WILLING TO WIN

ON THE MORNING OF JULY 28, 1984, the sun rose in a cloudless sky, promising a beautiful day for the Summer Olympic Games. Los Angeles was the host city, and the Olympic Village, at the University of California at Los Angeles (UCLA), was bursting with 8,000 athletes from 140 countries.

Although they came from different cultures, with a variety of languages and lifestyles, all were world-class athletes, and all shared a common goal. Each was bent on winning an Olympic medal—preferably the gold.

Among the competing athletes was a vivid, dark-skinned, 22-year-old woman named Jackie Joyner. This was her first Olympics, the culmination of a dream she had had since childhood.

The original Olympic Games took place about 3,000 years earlier, in ancient Greece, and were held in honor of the Greeks' most important god, Zeus. One of the first games was track, or foot races. In later years, other sports, such as chariot races, wrestling, boxing, discus throw, and javelin throw were added. The contestants and spectators came from cities and tribes all over Greece, sometimes from areas that were hostile to one another. But a truce was always declared during the Games; peace existed everywhere, everyone could travel safely, and no battles were fought.

The ancient Olympic Games were held every four years for about a thousand years, until A.D. 394, when the Roman emperor Theodosius, a Christian, abolished them because he believed they were pagan festivals.

In 1896, the first of the modern Olympic Games was held in Athens, Greece. Today the Summer and Winter Olympic Games still follow the traditions and goal of the ancient Games: they occur every four years; they are open to amateur athletes who meet in a spirit of friendly competition to determine who, regardless of nationality, is the best in the world; and their ultimate goal is to foster goodwill among nations.

The Olympic Games are hosted by a different country each time. Naturally, each host nation tries to outdo the previous hosts by trying to create the best, most exciting spectacle ever. The 1984 Summer Olympic Games, in which Jackie Joyner competed, were held in Los Angeles, California, and had all the glamour, expertise, and skill of Hollywood behind them.

Opening Day began with the Olympic Torch completing its relay from Greece to the Los Angeles Coliseum. Gina Hemphill, granddaughter of champion athlete Jesse Owens (winner of four gold medals in the 1936 Olympics), carried the torch into the Coliseum and then handed it to Rafer Johnson, the 1960 Olympic decathlon gold medalist. Johnson made a breathtaking ascent on an incredible moving stairway leading heavenward and then lit the Olympic Flame, which was kept burning day and night until the end of the Olympics.

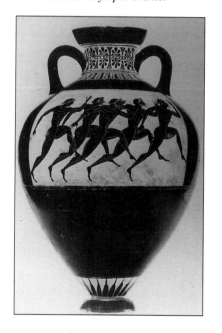

A Greek vase, an example of black-figure pottery from the 6th century B.C., *depicts runners in a race. The first Olympic Games were held in ancient Greece and were foot races. In later years, chariot races, wrestling, boxing, the discus throw, and the javelin throw, among other sports, became Olympic events.*

Next the sky was filled with the noise and smoke of rockets and fireworks bursting above the spectators, and with thousands of balloons of all colors. As the crowd clapped, the field came alive with 1,065 handpicked schoolgirls drilling in the sun; a magic show; people costumed so that they turned into flags; 184 pianists playing stirring American music; and a marching band that became a map of the United States, playing "America the Beautiful."

Then came the athletes, wearing handsome uniforms that were especially designed for the occasion in the colors of their native countries. They paraded behind the ramrod straight flag bearers, each of whom strode proudly, holding high their country's flag, which whipped briskly in an obliging breeze.

As each flag passed by the VIP box, it was dipped in honor of the courage and the ideals to which the Olympics are dedicated: peace and brotherhood. Only the U.S. flag was not dipped. With one exception, it has not dipped since 1908, when the Olympics were held in London, England. That year the U.S. flag bearer was a 6-foot-6-inch, 280-pound shot putter named Ralph Rose. No one knows for sure why he did not dip the flag but he may have been angry because the White City Stadium, in which he was marching, flew the flags of all participating countries except Sweden and the United States. (The American organizers said they could not find an American flag.)

From then on, the U.S. flag was not dipped until the 1932 Winter Olympic Games in Lake Placid, New York. Governor (later President) Franklin Roosevelt was in the VIP box, and bobsledder Billy Fiske lowered the flag as he passed Mr. Roosevelt. Asked why he broke with U.S. custom, Fiske said he thought it was the right and respectful thing to do.

Ten years later, Congress settled the question once and for all by passing Public Law 829, which makes it illegal to dip the U.S. flag. The law states, ". . . no disrespect should be given to the flag of the United States of America, the flag should not be dipped to any person or thing."

And then began the most exciting moment of all, the reason for all the pageantry and pomp, the Olympic Games themselves.

Even then the stadium is never still. During the Games, many events occur simultaneously, and the grandstand is alive with spectators who shout and wave flags wildly as they follow their favorite athletes. Some hold their collective breaths as they await the outcome of a race and the decisions of the judges. Others jump up and call out encouragement to spur on a popular athlete as he or she runs or jumps or makes a throw.

Jackie was delighted to be part of the Olympics at last. She had worked hard and practiced many long hours a day to get there. But she was confident, as usual, that she would do well. From the beginning, Jackie had been following a game plan she called her "three D's," determination, dedication, and desire. "I knew it would take more than my natural talent to succeed," she said. And for the past several years what she desired and determinedly dedicated herself to was reaching the ultimate, the Olympic gold medal.

Jackie's sport is the heptathlon, a grueling event that requires exceptional all-around athletic ability. It consists of seven separate track-and-field competitions that are counted as one event and are scored individually. It takes place over two consecutive days. At the end of the second day, all points for the seven events are added together for a cumulative total, and the heptathlete with the highest score wins.

To qualify for the Olympic Heptathlon Team, the nation's top athletes must compete in a national championship track meet called the Olympic Trials. Only the three highest-scoring athletes make the team.

Though Jackie had faced exceptionally tough competitors in the Trials, she had not only won, she had set a new American heptathlon record. So she looked forward

to the next two days with great expectations. Both Jackie and the sportswriters thought she had a good chance of winning.

She was especially excited and happy because her brother, Al, had made the U.S. Olympic Triple-Jump Team, and his event would be taking place at the same time as hers, just on the other side of the field. Jackie knew it was possible that she and her brother would both win an Olympic gold medal on the same day.

On the first day of the Olympic heptathlon the athletes compete in four events; the 100-meter hurdles, the high jump, the shot put, and the 200-meter dash. The second, and last, day belongs to the long jump, the javelin throw, and the 800-meter run.

If it sounds like an exhausting schedule, it is. The heptathlon is considered one of the most demanding events of the Olympics. Heptathletes barely get a breather

More than 1,000 helium balloons (each five feet high) are released during the opening ceremony of the 23rd Olympic Games in Los Angeles, California. The Games occur every four years and are meant to foster goodwill and peace among nations; amateur athletes compete to ascertain who is the best in their sport in the world.

between events, but that pace is exactly what Jackie likes. "The heptathlon was less boring than jumping," she says, explaining why she chose it. "I used to hate waiting around for the meet to end after my one little event was over."

One reason the heptathlon requires so much of an athlete is that the events are not similar; they call for sometimes incompatible skills. The running events demand speed and short, intense bursts of energy. The high jump demands flexibility and the ability to jump as high as possible. The long jump requires a controlled sprint to get on the narrow takeoff board without overstepping it, then springing up with a forward thrust, while keeping the legs extended widely apart in midair, and remaining poised in that position as long as possible for the longest landing distance. Jackie was a natural long jumper and she loved it.

The 100-meter hurdles, which call for a special running rhythm, had been a problem for Jackie at first because she had had trouble pacing herself. But her coach, Bob Kersee, had worked with her on the technique and she had mastered it.

The shot put and javelin are the hardest for a heptathlete to learn; they call for skills not used in running and jumping. For example, the shot put, which weighs 8 pounds 13 ounces, requires the kind of raw strength that interferes with flexibility, and the javelin is hard for the thrower to control because it moves idiosyncratically, yet must be thrown so that it hits the ground tip first. The first time Jackie tried to throw it, she hit herself in the head.

Jackie is a natural athlete but she has a disadvantage other heptathletes do not; she has asthma. Asthma is a chronic disease in which the body overreacts to everyday things, like cold weather, pollen, animal dander and saliva, foods, molds, and fungi. A reaction can also be brought on by an inflammation, a sinus infection, a cold, or exercise. These "triggers," as they are called, vary from person to person, even within a family. The reaction is usually an asthmatic attack; the air tubes (bronchial tubes) in the lungs narrow and fill with mucus, making it hard for a person to breathe.

The cause of asthma is still unknown, although it may be a combination of genetic predisposition and environmental factors. Considerable progress has been made in recent years in diagnosis and treatment, which emphasizes prevention rather than merely treating the symptoms. However, it can be serious, and presently about 3,000 to 4,000 Americans die of it every year.

A favorable aspect of asthma is that a person with the disease can be healthy and normal when not actually experiencing symptoms. In many cases, asthma is reversible and can be controlled.

Jackie's asthmatic trigger—the cause of her asthma—is exercise. She had gained recognition for her talent in spite of her problem, without even realizing she was different from other athletes. But a few years earlier, the more demanding training regimen of college sports had left her sometimes fighting for breath, and the college doctor had diagnosed the disease as asthma.

Jackie is now under a doctor's care, but even so, she knows she can still find herself unexpectedly gasping for breath in the middle of a race. Typically, she refuses to worry about getting sick. She simply follows her doctor's regimen: warming up slowly before exercise as well as cooling down afterward, routinely drinking large amounts of fluids, premedicating before strenuous activity, and taking her maintenance medications on schedule. In addition, any asthmatic subject to severe attacks is usually advised how to deal with them when they occur.

Most people with asthma, however, do not have to deal with the strict Olympic rules regarding drugs. These rules do not permit Joyner to use some of the drugs prescribed by her doctor that she should use to keep her asthma under control and, ideally, should take as a pretreatment just before an Olympic event.

As a result, Joyner must stop using these medications, which are a normal part of asthma maintenance and are used worldwide for that purpose, long enough before the Olympics so that the drug tests, routinely given to Olympic athletes, show no drugs in her system. Under these circumstances, it is not surprising that she often finishes an event, especially one as grueling as the 800-meter race, on her hands and knees gasping for breath.

An effort is being made to modify the Olympic rules to allow prescribed drugs such as these to be exempted from the rules. Meanwhile, Joyner does the best she can and concentrates on maintaining a positive attitude focusing on winning. This routine usually works.

On August 4, the beginning of the two-day Olympic heptathlon, Jackie Joyner was the odds-on favorite of the media and the crowd, and the focus of attention as she stretched and warmed up in preparation for the crucial contest ahead. When she stepped onto the field of the Olympic Stadium from the athletes' entrance, her fans erupted with shouts of "Jackie! Jackie!," and the stamping of thousands of pairs of feet shook the stands. Jackie was easy to spot because she had recently injured her left leg while training, and it was heavily bandaged. But a two-week crash program of physical therapy and extra rest had done wonders and she felt she was ready to win.

The atmosphere was electric with the anticipation of her cheering supporters, who were already imagining her mounting the winner's podium as the U.S. heptathlon Olympic gold medal winner. As the athletes streamed onto the oval track and the infield, Jackie, tall and slim in her red, white, and blue Olympic uniform, with no hint of her injury in her confident stride, smiled at her fans, clearly enjoying the moment and welcoming the demands of the exhausting two days she would face.

Jackie has always instinctively understood that, in addition to talent and training, becoming a champion requires a positive mind-set; to win you have to believe that you are going to win. Today athletes going into an event are taught to literally picture in their mind every one of the actual moves they are going to make, and to envision the end as a victory.

Bob Kersee, Jackie's coach, believes strongly in the importance of not allowing negative thoughts to drain an athlete's energy and confidence, and he always works on developing positive thinking, and on "walking through" a jump or run exactly the way it needs to go to get the best result. So Jackie's confidence ran deep.

One incident that had cast a damper on the 1984 Olympics had actually made victory more likely for Jackie. The Soviet Union and its allies were boycotting the 1984 Games in retaliation for the United States's boycott of the 1980 Games in Moscow. With the East German heptathletes literally out of the running, Jackie was the odds-on favorite, and the media and the fans were rooting for her.

But she knew she faced tough competition from Glynis Nunn of Australia. She had never actually competed against Nunn but she had read press reports of her prowess. Joyner later admitted that "[Coach Kersee] told me not to worry about her, just to do the best I could and that would be enough. . . . But I couldn't stop thinking about her."

The first day, Jackie finished the four events—100-meter hurdles, shot put, high jump, and 200-meter run—in second place. Being in second place did not worry her, she was sure she could make up the points. She looked forward to the second day, expecting to pick up a strong lead with a high-scoring long jump, which was usually her best event.

The long jump allows the athlete three chances, and only the score for the best jump counts. Jackie seldom needed more than one jump but now her injured leg threw off her stride, and she fouled the first two jumps by pushing off past the takeoff board. In her third (and last) try, she jumped poorly. Her score was still high compared to the other jumpers, and she ended up with a slight lead.

On August 4, 1984, Jackie Joyner (left) and her brother, Al, appear together after Jackie was awarded the silver medal in the heptathlon. Earlier in the day, Al had won the gold medal in the triple jump, making the two Joyners the first brother and sister to win medals at the Olympics on the same day.

Jackie's lead held through the javelin throw, but Nunn was inching up. The 800-meter run was next and last and Jackie knew she was far enough ahead in points so that she could even lose the run and still win the gold medal she so passionately desired. But it was a little tricky; she could lose but she could not lose by much. She would have to stay close to Nunn no matter what. Unfortunately, her leg was beginning to hurt and she was tiring.

On the other side of the stadium, Jackie's brother, Al Joyner, had completed three rounds out of the six attempts allowed in the triple-jump event. He was in the lead and had jumped outstandingly, beating his own personal best record by a wide margin.

He looked across the field to see how his sister was doing, and then, without a moment's hesitation, left his event just as the fourth round was beginning, and ran along the track oval just as Jackie was beginning the second lap of the two-lap run. Al saw that Nunn was pulling too far ahead and he ran alongside the oval track, yelling for his sister to stay close to her. "Pump your arms, Jackie. This is it!" Al shouted.

Jackie poured her waning strength into a speed burst but she was just a fraction of a second too slow. Nunn won the gold medal.

Al Joyner won the Olympic gold medal in the triple jump, the first American in 80 years to do so. Jackie won the silver in the heptathlon.

Jackie was thrilled for her brother, but her silver medal was a great disappointment, and she never forgot it. "I came up short because I was stubborn, hardheaded, a brat," she says, admitting she had let herself get dehydrated while sulking after a poor long-jump showing. "Now I have a clipping of the names of the gold, silver and bronze medalists: Glynis Nunn, Jackie Joyner, Sabine Evert. I have that by my bed reminding me. . . ."

Another athlete would have been happy to win an Olympic silver medal. But Joyner had set her heart on the gold. She would have to wait until 1988, four more years, and now she was more determined than ever to win it.

Gateway Arch (center) in St. Louis, Missouri, which is located directly across the Mississippi River from Jackie's hometown of East St. Louis, Illinois, is seen in the distance in this photograph of grimy Trendley Avenue in East St. Louis. Jackie grew up in an economically depressed area of the city.

2

THE EARLY YEARS

IN 1962, THE TOWN of East St. Louis, Illinois, across the Mississippi River from the larger city of St. Louis, Missouri, had fallen on hard times. And the heart of its depressed ghetto district seemed like the least likely place to spawn an Olympic champion.

But the Joyner family, who resided in the ghetto, were good Baptists; they had faith that people could always somehow manage and make the most of what they had. Within their small family circle, they created a world of their own, always hopeful, if not positively optimistic.

So on March 3, 1962, when a baby girl was born in the small wooden house on Piggott Street, Ollie Mae Johnson—her maternal great grandmother—named her Jacqueline, after First Lady Jacqueline Kennedy, President John F. Kennedy's wife, and predicted "Someday this girl will be the first lady of something." Even Mrs. Johnson could not have dreamed how true her prediction would turn out to be.

At the time, the family's situation was not favorable. Alfred and Mary Joyner had married as teenagers, when Alfred was 14 and Mary was 16. At the time of the wedding, she was pregnant with their first child, Alfred Erick, and two years later Jackie was born. Angela and Debra followed soon after and the family settled down to coping with the difficult conditions in which they found themselves.

Mr. Joyner had been a promising pole vaulter and hurdler at Lincoln High School, near where they now lived, but he could not try for the athletic college scholarship he might have won because he had to drop out of school to support his family. Without even a high school diploma, he had to take whatever work he could get. He shined

A view of the southeast corner of 17th and Piggott streets in East St. Louis shows the neighborhood in which Jackie was born on March 3, 1962. Her parents, Mary and Alfred Joyner, were married as teenagers and worked hard to support their growing family.

shoes, mowed lawns, and welcomed whatever other odd jobs he could find. Fortunately, Mrs. Joyner was able to supplement the family's budget by working as a nurse's assistant at St. Mary's Hospital, while Great Grandmother Johnson took care of the children.

In spite of the parents' hard work, the Joyners were very, very poor. Every penny had to be spent carefully, but even then there were times when there was not enough to cover all their needs. Jackie had few clothes; she wore the same dress to school two days in a row, and her one pair of shoes had to make do until they wore out.

Although the house was small, it was hard to keep it warm, with only the kitchen stove for heat during the cold East St. Louis winters. On the chilliest nights, the whole family simply slept in the kitchen. And often there was little or no food to eat, with dinner consisting of bread and mayonnaise.

Through it all the adults kept up the family's spirits and were very supportive. The children were brought up to be cheerful and to be thankful for what they had. "We didn't think we were poor," Jackie Joyner recalled. "We didn't have a lot, but we knew our mother and father were doing their best."

Happily, the Joyner home was just around the corner from the Mary E. Brown Community Center. It was a wonderful place for children and young adults, with many varied sports and recreation programs and even a swimming pool. Jackie learned the joy of personal achievement at the Center, and its activities kept her off the surrounding ghetto streets, where there was a constant threat of danger and violence. Years later, Jackie was to give money to the Center so that other children could enjoy the same benefits that she had had.

Al Joyner became the first in the family to make use of the Center, joining the swimming and diving programs. After seeing the fun her brother was having, Jackie joined too. Because she was tall, long-legged, and a naturally fast

This 1968 picture depicts Collinsville Avenue, the major commercial street of East St. Louis, which during its heyday in the late 19th century was called the "Pittsburgh of the West." Because many of its chief industries closed between 1950 and 1964, East St. Louis lost almost half of its population when residents were forced to move elsewhere to find jobs.

runner, Jackie gravitated toward the Center's track-and-field team. In addition, she took lessons in dance and acting.

"At the time," she related years later, "dance was my first love. The instructor cared for me a lot, and felt that one day I would be on Broadway." Jackie was excited by this encouragement. She immediately took this potential

new career seriously and, with her sisters and friends, formed a dance group called the Fabulous Dolls.

But this budding career came to a sudden halt when her dance instructor unexpectedly died; somehow Jackie just did not have the heart to continue. Not one to endure a vacuum for long, she threw all her energy and ambition into track and field.

As so often happens in life, what seemed like a major disappointment and setback was probably the best thing that could have happened to Jackie at that time. And, following in his younger sister's footsteps, Al began to concentrate on track and field, too. It turned out to be a crucial choice for both of them.

Looking back at her career, it sometimes seems as though luck always smiled on Jackie just when she needed it. Early on, it surfaced in the person of Coach Nino Fennoy. Coach Fennoy was deeply involved in the neighborhood because he had grown up there and had participated in the track-and-field team at nearby Lincoln High School. After his graduation from Tennessee State University, his loyalty to the area brought him back to coach the Center's track-and-field program. Thanks to his stewardship, it was now reputed to be one of the best city programs in the entire country.

Even at the age of nine, Jackie had a way of standing out from the crowd. But Coach Fennoy's first impression of her had nothing to do with her sports ability. What stood out about her, he explained some years later, was "just the happiness. She wanted to be doing what we were doing. I can still see her head with the pigtails, the little skinny legs, the knees, and the smile." With all her intensity, this was what everyone always noticed about Jackie; she loved what she was doing, whatever it was, and always gave it her best shot.

Her first track competition gave little indication of her future greatness. She had joined the East St. Louis Railers, Fennoy's track-and-field club for elementary and junior high students, and was running in the Junior Olympics Regionals, which included athletes from ages 9 to 18. In her age group, she was rated only the fourth or fifth fastest girl, and although she won a ribbon in the regionals, she finished last.

True to her burgeoning philosophy of life, she refused to get discouraged and simply made up her mind to do better next time. This perseverance and determination to ultimately win was to characterize Jackie in all her future contests. As she said of this first taste of defeat, "I decided that this was a challenge and that I was going to do my best."

Deciding to do "her best" was not just an exercise in boundless optimism. Joyner had been taught by her parents that one had to work to get what one wanted out of life, and she had accepted that as a given from an early age. Although she attracted the attention of coaches because of her stick-to-it-iveness and joy in what she was doing, they also saw in her the qualities that usually must exist to create a champion. Coach Fennoy described the special qualities Jackie displayed even at this early age, "She came to practice. She had respect for adults, and discipline, and an air of enjoyment, like, 'My parents sent me here to have

The Mary Brown Community Center was located around the corner from Jackie's home. Al Joyner joined the swimming and diving programs at the center, and soon after, Jackie enrolled in the track-and-field program and in dance and acting classes.

some fun and learn some things.' She wasn't in a hurry, she never complained."

Like all coaches, Fennoy was always on the lookout for that once-in-a-lifetime winner, a young athlete who showed a gleam of that indefinable star quality. He thought he saw this possibility in Joyner. "With Jackie, it's like she had the gift. When I'm speaking of gift, it's not just the athletic portion. She had the mental attitude, the spiritual attitude, to weather the ups and downs."

She also had another quality that distinguishes a winning athlete—she was open to, and willing to take, advice from coaches. All good coaches are tough taskmasters; they constantly strive to bring out the best in their athletes, and they do not settle for less than an all-out effort. Only a truly committed athlete can take the intensity of the training.

Coach Fennoy was no exception. He took Jackie and her training seriously in spite of her youth. He began grooming her for the big time he saw in her future. "Where you're going, you'll need to express yourself with more than your legs and arms," he explained. He began training her not only in sports skills but also in the skills she would need to cope with the life he envisioned for her. She even had to keep journals on the team's road trips, which he corrected for grammar and spelling.

In the beginning, her track-and-field career got off to a slow start, but she had endless patience with practicing and never envied the athletes who won the contests she continued to lose. "There was no jealously or animosity," Fennoy recalled. "She appreciated the accomplishments of others and used that as fuel to become a better person and athlete."

Jackie and her brother were very close all through their childhood as well as later in life. They were happy competitors, constantly teasing and egging each other on to greater achievement. Because both were now into track and field, this became an arena of challenge. Al was the big brother; all of two years older, he felt he had an edge. One day, when he was 12, he got overconfident and blithely said he could beat Jackie in a race without practicing. Jackie took up the challenge and agreed to the contest. But she had not said *she* would not practice, so she buckled down to prepare. She practiced faithfully every day until the race.

The race course had been established as the distance from the mailbox on their street corner to the fence in front of their house, about 70 yards. All the neighborhood children and their friends turned out to watch the race. But to Al's surprise and chagrin, Jackie won.

Of course, she immediately felt sorry. "I felt kind of bad. I was a girl beating a boy, and Al's friends started calling him names. But by beating Al, I let him know that I wasn't a push-around. And he learned to respect me as an athlete." This was an unusually mature attitude for a 10-year-old girl, but it revealed both the compassion for her competitors and the strong sense of self-worth that was to be evident in Jackie again and again in her later years.

Jackie was always open to new sports. The coach had her training for the 400-meter run, but she wanted to try the long jump. "He had other girls jumping and I just had to sit around and wait. One day, a young lady was late to practice, so I just ran down the runway and jumped." She took off at a run with her pigtails flying, leapt into a new sand pit that one of the coaches was building, and jumped almost 17 feet. The coach watched in amazement; though only 12 years old, she had jumped as far as a high school athlete. He asked whether she could do it again. So she did. She said he looked at her and replied, "You've been this good all this time." Jackie later explained, "It was something I had always wanted to do, and it was taken away from me, and I got a chance by accident. The following year, I set a record of 17 feet for 12- and 13-year-olds."

That was the beginning of her lifelong love of the long jump. Characteristically, she set about becoming as expert as possible in her newly discovered sport. She practiced constantly, whenever and wherever she could. Because Jackie did not always have a sand pit available, she improvised, even utilizing her porch at home.

Although she was devoting most of her sports time to track and field, Jackie took advantage of other opportunities at the Center. She tried basketball and volleyball and discovered she loved playing as part of a team. Because she never felt a need to hog the limelight, she got along well with the other players and worked for the good of all instead of trying to outdo others. It became increasingly evident that Jackie was a natural athlete and that her basic skills were applicable to various fields.

Coach Fennoy, watching her develop, quickly picked up on the flexibility of his potential star. He encouraged her to try competing in the pentathlon, where her jumping and running ability would give her a head start over competitors.

The pentathlon is a single sport consisting of five events. In addition to an 800-meter race, it includes hurdles, putting the shot, the long jump, and the high jump. The pentathlon athlete has to compete in all five and the winning score is calculated by combining the scores from the five events according to a special pentathlon formula.

Through the pentathlon, Jackie was introduced to another world. She had to learn how to jump over hurdles, a technique that did not come naturally to her because the hurdles required developing a new pacing of her stride and of timing, to which she had never been exposed and which she found difficult to master. In fact, it was not until years later that she finally overcame the problems she had with jumping hurdles.

She also had to master the shot put, in which the athlete tries to "throw" a metal ball, weighing 8 pounds 13 ounces, farther than her competitors. It requires spinning in place to generate the power to heave it from one's hand, and none of the skills Jackie had learned in running and jumping were of any help in this ancient sport.

As always, Jackie Joyner joyfully rose to the new challenges. She was growing up, and the more she practiced, the more control she developed. The change was noticeable and it was not lost on Coach Fennoy. "Those were explosive years for her. It's as if someone pushed a button and said, 'It's your time.'"

Wearing her Lincoln High School Tigerettes sweats, Jackie stretches before a track meet in 1978. By the age of 16, Jackie had already proved to be an Illinois high school state champion runner and a national champion in the pentathlon.

3

A GLIMPSE OF GLORY

AT THE AGE OF 14, Jackie Joyner discovered the Olympics. It was, apparently, the first time she thought of the Games as an event relating to her own life. Suddenly she glimpsed the possibility of actually reaching the rarefied heights of a world-class athlete. As she watched Bruce Jenner on television win the gold medal in the decathlon in Montreal, Quebec, during the 1976 Olympic Games, she realized she was seeing an event similar to the pentathlon, a sport to which her coach had steered her, and in which she was currently competing. (The decathlon consists of 10 events: the 100-meter, 400-meter, and 1,500-meter runs, the 110-meter high hurdles, the javelin and discuss throws, shot put, pole vault, high jump, and long jump.) Quietly but confidently, she privately predicted to Al, "One day I'm going to go to the Olympics," and she did not mean as a spectator.

On July 30, 1976, Bruce Jenner (right) clears the 110-meter hurdles in the fourth heat during the decathlon competition at the Olympics in Montreal, Quebec. After Jenner won the gold medal in the decathlon, with a total of 8,618 points, Jackie told her brother that she, too, would someday compete in a multievent at the Olympics.

This was not just a teenager's fantasy. She had been brought up to work for what she wanted, and from that day on, she set her sights on the Olympics and devoted her considerable energies to training for her ambitious new goal.

Joyner's determination and perseverance quickly brought results, and in 1976 she tried out and qualified for the pentathlon event at the National Junior Olympics. However, as always, money was a problem. The location of the competition was a car trip away and neither she nor her teammates could afford it. But they had grown up having to find their own money for such "frills," so they

went about fund-raising in traditional small-town ways, through neighborhood bake and penny-candy sales, and saving what they could out of their lunch money. Finally they raised enough money to make the trip, and they were on their way. Joyner's expectations ran high and, as usual, she looked forward to a new experience and challenge with great confidence.

The result was a precursor of deeds to come; Joyner won the national championship, with the highest pentathlon score in her 13- to 14-year-old age group.

Most great athletes were inspired early in life by the examples set by others and Joyner did not have to look far for her role models. She had learned about Wilma Rudolph from Coach Fennoy, who was friends with the coach who had discovered and trained Rudolph. Rudolph, an African American who was crippled by polio at the age of four, was an Olympic gold medalist in track and field, and had overcome the daunting obstacles of health, poverty, and racism to become "The Tennessee Tornado," whom the sports world called the fastest woman on earth. A former high school basketball and track star, Rudolph earned an athletic scholarship to college, won her first Olympic medal, a bronze, in 1956 when she was 16, and won her three Olympic gold medals four years later. Rudolph's path to success was one Joyner saw possible for herself if she worked hard. She knew Fennoy thought in those terms for her, and she saw the road to glory that Rudolph had trod now stretching before her.

Joyner also greatly admired Mildred "Babe" Didrikson (later Zaharias), the acclaimed Olympic gold medalist in track and field, whom Joyner had watched in a television documentary. Didrikson was an exceptionally versatile athlete who competed successfully in many different sports. In the 1932 Olympics, she won gold medals in the 80-meter hurdles and the javelin, and a silver medal in the high jump. She was already immortalized in sports history as one of the greatest women athletes of all time. "Seeing

Wilma Rudolph runs through the tape in the 400-meter relay to win the event for the U.S. team at the 1960 Olympics in Rome, Italy. Called the "Tennessee Tornado," Rudolph won three gold medals at the 1960 Games; her success inspired Joyner to work hard to achieve her own goal to become an Olympic champion.

Babe run the hurdles and play baseball, golf, and basketball was something! She was a very tough woman and I admired her," Joyner said.

Joyner was a pretty tough woman herself. At this early age, she had already developed the single-mindedness that is one of the keys to success if one aspires to scale the heights of the sports spectrum. "It was a struggle," she said, speaking of her early efforts, but her willing-to-work philosophy and the always present "three D's," formed a bedrock that sustained her.

With her goals now more concretely in sight, she concentrated her energies even more than before. She prioritized her activities according to what would be most useful in reaching her dream. Even though she needed the money, she gave up her part-time job in a movie theater, and quit the cheerleading team so as to have more time for track and field, basketball, and volleyball. As an investment in the future, her choices could not have been better.

Her reputation as a young athlete was already high when she hit the big time at the 1977 National Junior Olympics, at the age of 15; she won by such a wide margin that the "Faces in the Crowd" section of *Sports Illustrated* featured her photograph and name.

All in all, Joyner won four consecutive National Junior Pentathlon Championships, proving, as she often did from then on, that she was not only good but that she was *consistently* good. She also continued to work on her other events, and, from then on, Joyner began breaking track-and-field and long-jump records so regularly that she was often competing against herself, trying to break the last record she had set. No one else could keep up with her.

She greeted entrance to high school in 1977 with the same enthusiasm with which she had welcomed other new experiences. Fortunately, Coach Fennoy was coach of Lincoln High's girls' track-and-field team so Joyner entered 10th grade with her mentor already in place. She lost no time in joining his team, as well as the volleyball and basketball teams.

Nino Fennoy had helped a number of students win college track scholarships and he knew what was needed to be successful in that endeavor. Joyner was a high school coach's ideal, not only a talented young athlete but also one who actually enjoyed combining a demanding training schedule with quality schoolwork. He recalled later that

joyfulness was as much a part of Jackie Joyner as her drive
to win. In high school, she was known for her irrepressible
humor and sense of fun. Because of her love of practical
jokes, her family and friends nicknamed her "The Joker."

High school sports were a big change from junior high,
with much greater competition from other athletes. But
with her long legs, speed, and height of 5 feet 10 inches,
she was a natural for the position of forward on the basketball team. And she was lucky in that the team was
already a good one. In fact, in the 1977–78 season it was
expected to win the Illinois state championship.

In the sectional semifinals, from which the winning
team would go to the state finals, something unexpected
happened. With Lincoln holding a strong lead, and Centralia High struggling to catch up, the gymnasium lights
went out.

An unplanned break in the middle of a game is always
dangerous because a certain amount of letdown and lost
momentum is almost inevitable, but only very experienced
players realize it. Lincoln was so far ahead that the young
players, thinking their win was in the bag, relaxed and
simply waited for play to start again. The more experienced Centralia knew the danger in inactive muscles. They
worked out and planned their plays, and did whatever they
could to hold their energy level at playing pitch.

As a result, when the lights went on, Lincoln found itself
completely disoriented. They had lost the cohesion and
fever pitch of a playing team, and they played as individuals instead of working off one another. In contrast, Centralia was still up to form; they were raring to go and they
did, right to the winning score.

Lincoln lost not only the game but a good deal of their
spirit. They had trouble putting the shock of the loss behind
them and it colored their play for the rest of the year.
Joyner, however, characteristically turned it into a learning
experience. She realized that they had lost because their
teamwork had fallen apart. She says today that it taught

Babe Didrikson jumps hurdles at an amateur track meet in the early 1930s. An extraordinarily versatile athlete, Didrikson was an All-American basketball player, and broke several records in the 1932 Olympics, winning three medals (two golds and one silver) in track and field. Joyner admired Didrikson's skill in sports and her tough competitiveness.

her that if a team is to win, the members must work like a well-oiled piece of machinery, each one doing its part toward the whole endeavor. "I learned to ask myself whether I was doing the things that were in my best interest and in the best interest of the team. And I learned that as a leader, I had to be willing to make the same demands on my teammates," she explained.

Joyner took her leadership role as seriously as she had taken all her other achievements, and said, "Sometimes my teammates would get mad at me or tease me because I confronted them or told the coach if I thought someone was doing something that could stop the team from winning, like hanging out with a boyfriend instead of going to practice. That didn't make me too popular at first, but after a while my teammates respected me for doing it. They knew that it would help us become champions."

She continued to grow in her chosen sports. In 1979, Joyner became captain of the volleyball team, and her

Joyner attended East St. Louis's Lincoln High School. In 1979, she became captain of the volleyball and basketball teams.

performance on the basketball court was nothing short of outstanding. She is still remembered for a game she won with a shot she sank from 25 feet away in the final second of play. In her senior year, the Lincoln girls' basketball team, under her captaincy, won the state championship.

What Joyner was actually doing, of course, was emulating the good coaching she had received, accepted, and benefited from. She was passing on to her teammates the discipline that was to take her to the top. "When she was the captain of the team," said one of her teammates, Carmen Cannon-Taylor, "it was 'Get your butt up, we're gonna run.' If you do 100 percent, she'll do 120 percent. We were all disciplined, but she was more disciplined."

Meanwhile, she was not neglecting her favorite sport, track and field. Thanks to her, and Coach Fennoy's inspired coaching, the track team won three state titles, and she established a state high school long-jump record of 20 feet 7½ inches in the spring of 1979 and was named All-State and All-American in both track and basketball.

In addition, she had benefited from the close, uncompromising male companionship of her brother, Al, who was big and strong and never coddled her. "When I played with my little sister, I had to be physically rough to beat her," Al admitted.

Everything that was happening reinforced the confidence she had always had and that never seemed to fail her. Her friend Carmen tells of an occasion when they were introduced to the athlete who held the record in the women's long jump. Joyner said to her, "How are you? I'm going to beat your record." Carmen tried to explain to Jackie that one should not talk to people like that. But Jackie said simply, "It's only the truth." And, of course, it was.

Although she did so well in schoolwork and in sports, Joyner still faced the temptations and dangers of the neighborhood in which she was growing up. While she was still in grade school, her father had to take a job working for the railroad. It meant a two-hour commute to work and less time spent with the family, and it put the burden of raising the children on her mother's shoulders.

Mary Joyner loved her children and so she was strict with them. She felt she had made a bad mistake allowing herself to become pregnant while she was still a teenager and she was determined that her children would not follow in her footsteps. She wanted a better life for them than the one she had and she kept after them to do their schoolwork and to resist the temptations of bad companions and the ways of the neighborhood. Joyner had already seen a man shot right on their street, so her mother's fears were not unrealistic.

Mrs. Joyner emphasized that Jackie was never to hang around talking to boys, and made her come home every night before dark. "Both my folks were frightened of boys," Jackie remembers, "My mother said, with no chance for negotiation, that I was not going out with guys until I was 18." She appreciated what her mother was trying to do for them. "My mother was the foundation. She didn't want us to be like her—not getting what she wanted because she couldn't go to college. She wanted us to find a way out. So I threw myself into sports and school."

By her senior year, her ability had outgrown the Junior Olympics, and she was asked to try out for the real thing, the Olympic Trials for the 1980 Olympic Long Jump Team. She more than earned this unusual invitation—high school students are seldom invited to such a tryout—by jumping a personal best of 20 feet 9¾ inches, which put her in the record books for all time. But she did not make the team.

Her disappointment was not as great as it might have been because the United States withdrew from the 1980 Olympics and no American athletes participated that year. U.S. president Jimmy Carter boycotted the Olympic Games, which were to be held in Moscow, because the Soviet Union had invaded Afghanistan, an act that many countries, including the United States, saw as a violation of international law. The repercussions of this boycott were to affect future Olympics and have an unexpected result on Joyner's career.

In 1980, all of Joyner's hard work and self-discipline paid off in a big way. She graduated from high school in the top 10 percent of her class, and this strong academic standing, plus her exceptional sports record, attracted basketball scholarship offers from numerous colleges. Of course, she would rather have had a track-and-field scholarship, but basketball scholarships were easier to come by, and she was more of a star in that sport. Also, she knew that getting into college on any kind of a scholarship was the first step, and she could negotiate better once she was on campus. Joyner understood very well the momentum

Hoping to recruit Jackie for the women's basketball team at the University of California, Los Angeles, Coach Billie Moore visited Jackie four times in East St. Louis. Jackie was offered a basketball scholarship at UCLA, which she accepted.

involved in taking one step at a time, and she had all the patience in the world when she needed it.

It was hard to decide among the various schools, especially because her friends and family did not usually go on to college and could not advise her. She finally chose the University of California in Los Angeles (UCLA) because it was known for the quality of its coaches, and she realized she needed the best professional coaching help she could get if she was to hone her skills to Olympic standards. Its basketball team was one of the best in the country, and it did not hurt that UCLA's coach, Billie Moore, came to East St. Louis four times to persuade her to choose UCLA.

In the fall of 1980, Jackie Joyner exchanged the cold and mean streets of her East St. Louis home for the warmth, palm trees, and glamour of Los Angeles, California. She was going to college!

As a UCLA sophomore, Joyner shattered her collegiate record in the heptathlon with 6,099 points at the National Collegiate Athletic Association Outdoor Track and Field championships. At the time, her performance was the third best in history by an American.

4

A WHOLE NEW WORLD

THE COLLEGE SCENE was a whole new and not entirely comfortable world for Joyner. Even her beloved sports revealed much that was strange and unfamiliar. Transported from Lincoln High School, where she was known, loved, and respected, to the sprawling campus full of overachievers to whom she was a complete stranger, she felt traumatized. Fortunately the college had guided many a freshman through the initial shock and, to make it easier for Joyner, they had also recruited Deborah Thurston, who had been her teammate and friend in high school.

But Joyner had firmly hitched her wagon to her star, and it guided her unerringly through this strange new land. Even before she enrolled in the fall of 1980, while she was still negotiating the terms of her scholarship with Coach Billie Moore, she had kept her eye on her future. While accepting the scholarship with gratitude and enthusiasm,

she managed to persuade the coach to let her also go out
for track and field. Of course, the fact that so many colleges
were vying for this bright young athlete gave her bargain-
ing power. Even so, such a concession would not ordinar-
ily have been permitted because she was being admitted
on a *basketball* scholarship.

Colleges were usually reluctant to let new students take
on the extra work of a second sport because, in their
experience, the students would have their hands full just
meeting the academic requirements and the sports commitment the scholarship required. And UCLA was not the sort
of college to let even a star athlete shirk the academic side.
But Joyner had already demonstrated an ability to deal
with the complexities of her dual dedication to sports and
to quality schoolwork. So when she promised not to let her
track-and-field work interfere with basketball games or
practices, Moore reluctantly agreed she could go out for
the extra sport.

Joyner's college basketball career got off to a slow start.
Her performance on the court was spectacularly uneven.
One sportswriter quoted a fan, speaking in amazement and
trepidation, "She's fast and wild." But she got it out of her
system in record time and settled down as a four-year
starter on the Lady Bruins. She soon ranked among the
all-time Top 10 Lady Bruins in assists, rebounding, and
scoring.

Coach Moore was delighted that her new recruit so
quickly justified her judgment. Not only was Joyner a
crackerjack rebounder, she was also a no-holds-barred
defensive player, and, best of all, she never hogged the
limelight but consistently worked for the good of the team.
Lincoln High School had done its job well.

But Joyner was still a small fish in a very big pond.
Whereas she had stood out from the crowd at Lincoln
High, at UCLA she was, initially, just another good athlete
among many. And the fact that she was on a basketball
scholarship tended to stereotype her. What this meant, in

Joyner (number 23) goes up for a shot. Although her basketball career started off sluggishly, Joyner buckled down, and she soon ranked among the all-time Top 10 Bruin scorers.

practical terms, was that the other coaches were inclined not to take her desire to go out for track and field seriously.

Joyner found that she was looked upon as "a walk-on," a student who just happens to walk on the field where a sport is being trained, and tries out for the team more or less on an impulse. No one takes walk-ons seriously, least of all busy coaches trying to put together a winning team.

In addition, UCLA has an impressive sports program and a large roster of coaches. Prior to attending UCLA, she had to make an impression on just the one coach the high school had. Here she was suddenly confronted with a number of coaches, and no way to attract any one coach's full attention. Even though the coaches tried to help her as much as they had time to, she could not count on always getting the same one two days in a row. One day she would get some advice on her work, and the next day an entirely different coach would give her entirely different advice. It was confusing and upsetting to a shy freshman from a small town, but Joyner had come up the hard way and she never expected anything to be easy.

Instead of giving up and going away, she did just what she had done in East St. Louis, Illinois. She chose her first love, the long jump, and simply practiced it by herself over and over on the field where the other athletes were practicing. Unfortunately, instead of improving, her jumping began to deteriorate.

But once again her persistence paid off. Bob Kersee, who had joined the faculty in 1980 as the new assistant coach of women sprinters and hurdlers, somehow noticed her. He was not a long-jump coach but he saw she was having difficulty and he knew enough to recognize that her problem was lack of technique. He could see that physically she had the potential to be a good long jumper. "I saw this talent walking around the campus that everyone was blind to. No one was listening to her mild requests to do more."

Joyner knew Kersee was a sprinter/hurdler coach and felt she should be coached by him. Kersee commented that he thought she was intimidated by him because she could hear him yelling at his athletes across the field. But Joyner said that, on the contrary, she wished she had a coach who cared enough to yell at her.

When Kersee began to work with Joyner, he found she had even more ability than he had initially thought. It seemed to him she could do better by not concentrating on just one event, like the long jump, but switching to a multievent sport. He knew how quickly she had mastered the pentathlon, achieving championship status in the Junior Olympics in record time, so he was confident she was ready to scale even greater heights.

At the time, UCLA did not have an assistant coach for women's multievents so Kersee asked Dr. Judith Holland, the women's athletic director, for permission to take on that additional assignment. Kersee is a tough coach and he was willing to put his job on the line for an athlete he believed in as strongly as he had come to believe in Jackie Joyner. His conversation with Dr. Holland, he later reported, was, "Either I coached her in the hurdles, long jump, and multievents, or I'd quit, because to go on as she had would be an abuse of her talent."

Dr. Holland asked Joyner how she felt about this new venture. What Bob Kersee had in mind was the heptathlon, a seven-event competition, that had just been created by adding two more sports, the javelin and the 800-meter race, to the pentathlon, and that would be an Olympic sport in 1984. As usual, Joyner welcomed the idea of a new challenge. Much as she loved the long jump, it entailed a lot of waiting around between turns; with the heptathlon there would be a lot more action. Also, she had enjoyed the pentathlon, and this new coach's ideas might get her to the Olympic Games.

The first semester of her freshman year sped by and soon it was Christmas. Joyner had made a host of new friends and she chose to spend the holidays with them instead of going back to East St. Louis. But, as it happened, she was soon to return under unhappy circumstances.

Her beloved mother, whom she worshipped, and who had always guided her safely through the difficulties of the family's lives, died unexpectedly of meningitis (an inflammation of one or all of the membranes that encase the brain and the spinal cord; it is usually caused by a bacterial infection) in January 1981, at the age of 38.

Throughout Jackie's childhood, her mother, Mary, working as a nurse's assistant in a nearby hospital, had kept the family together even during a trying time when Mr. Joyner had become an alcoholic and a somewhat upsetting influence in the household. A tribute in a subsequent article in *Life* magazine said, "It was from Mary that [Jackie] learned a kind of old-fashioned decency that encompassed a host of values—modesty, faith, perseverance—that seems almost anachronistic today, especially in the bitter cynical ghetto where she was raised."

By the time Joyner and her brother, Al, who was attending Arkansas State University, arrived home, their mother was in a coma, and she was dying. The doctors said they could keep her alive if they put her on life-support machines but that the disease had already destroyed her brain, and there was no chance that she would ever come out of the coma and regain consciousness.

Mary Joyner had once said she would not want to be kept alive just by machines, but her husband could not face turning off her life-support system. Brokenhearted as she was, Jackie faced up to carrying out her mother's wishes. "If we left her on the machines," she said, "she'd never have known us, and she would have suffered indefinitely."

With Mrs. Joyner gone, the family had to make some adjustments. It was out of the question for either Al or Jackie to stay home, so they returned to college, leaving an aunt, Della Gaines, who had offered to take charge, to care for their two younger sisters, Angela and Debra.

Joyner, faced with the most devastating moment in her life up to that time, reacted stoically. Instead of grieving openly, she kept it inside herself and tried to go on at college without showing her sorrow. Not sharing her feelings made it twice as hard to deal with them and it seemed there was no one to show her how to cope.

Unexpected help came from Bob Kersee who heard about Jackie's mother's death and was able to sympathize because he had lost his own mother nine years before, when he was only 18 years old.

Joyner was surprised at his warmth and caring. "I found it amazing because I didn't know him beyond his being a coach. But he said if I had doubts and needed to talk them out, I could come to him." The doubts Kersee was con-

Al Joyner was attending Arkansas State University when he heard the news that his mother had meningitis. By the time he and Jackie reached Mary Joyner's bedside, she had lapsed into a coma. Their mother's death made the bond between Jackie and Al even stronger than before.

cerned about were whether Joyner would feel she had to drop out of school to take care of her sisters now that she was the oldest woman in the family. "I tried to protect her from the 'Now I'm the mom' syndrome," he said later.

Joyner probably could not have had a better person to help her through this sad period in her life. Not only had Bob Kersee undergone a similar experience but his frame of reference was, naturally, sports, and because Joyner's interest in sports was also paramount in her life, it was the perfect way to offer her solace, distract her from her grief, and keep her too busy to brood on her loss. The challenge of the heptathlon came into her life at exactly the right time.

Although it meant a crash course in the so-called technical events, the javelin and the shot put, Joyner took to the heptathlon like a duck to water. She did not need to master the two technicals to the degree that she had jumping and running, but she was such a versatile athlete that she still managed very well. Because the heptathlon consisted of seven events that were scored as one, her exceptional ability in, for instance, the long jump, more than made up for a slight weakness in any of the other events.

Furthermore, she had quality coaching to bring out her best. Kersee not only coached her in the right way to do each event, how to utilize her strengths—her long legs and her speed—and how to minimize her weaknesses, he taught her that winning involved strategy, the ability to *think* sports. He showed her how to analyze each heptathlon event in terms of her abilities; to judge where she was most likely to get the most points and where she had to work extra hard, as in the hurdles, javelin, and shot put. She understood perfectly and later explained, "I enjoyed doing different events and not trying to single one out. But I needed to work on all my events, especially the technical events." Instinct and natural ability alone would no longer get her where she wanted to go, but Kersee showed her how she could still control her destiny by planning ahead.

Joyner soars through the air in the long jump, one of her best events. Joyner took to the heptathlon instantly, but she also had expert coaching from Bob Kersee, who taught her how to make use of her strengths.

Meanwhile, in the spring of her freshman year, 1981, Joyner qualified for her first heptathlon competition at the Association of Intercollegiate Athletics for Women National Championships in Tacoma, Washington. When Kersee discovered no coach was assigned to accompany her, he angrily said he was going to go even if he had to pay his own way. UCLA agreed to pay Kersee for the trip and it later proved to be well worthwhile.

The power of good coaching was soon evident. The evening after the first day of the event, with Joyner behind in the scoring, Kersee said, "Girl, you have a lot of talent. You're going to be one of the best heptathletes."

The first event of the next day was Joyner's best, the long jump. Kersee created a long-jump runway with masking tape in the motel hall, and Joyner used the improvised space to work on her approach and takeoff—just as enthusiastically as she had practiced from the porch of her house when she was only 12 years old.

The improvised field worked beautifully. The next morning she jumped the farthest distance she had achieved since high school: 21 feet. All told, she finished the heptathlon in a respectable third place.

Joyner ended her freshman year with mixed emotions. It had been a time of great change and growth, and her performance on the basketball court had more than justified her scholarship, but she was still a little disappointed with her progress in track.

In the mean time, her asthma had surfaced and was interfering with the intense practices that college athletics required. Because her condition had never been diagnosed and she had never paid any particular attention to her symptoms or to the asthma attacks, they took her by surprise. She would find that she simply had to stop whatever she was doing, often gasping for breath and doubling over, to try to get more air into her suddenly tightened lungs.

Naturally, she was frightened. However, the doctor soon explained the problem and told her that many athletes had asthma and had learned to manage it and continue to compete successfully. Because her asthma is brought on by exercise, it will never disappear completely and cannot be cured.

Not so many years ago, it was thought that children with asthma should sit on the sidelines and never participate in sports. Asthmatic children were pictured as pale and thin, racked by wheezing, and only able to watch others run and play. Fortunately, doctors now know that exercise is actually good for asthmatics, and world-class champions like diver Greg Louganis and swimmer Nancy Hogshead have proved it is no obstacle to athletic achievement. Joyner would have to manage her asthma, but she did not have to let it stop her. And she did not—sophomore year found her hitting her stride.

On May 31, 1983, Joyner long jumps 21 feet 3/4 inches at the NCAA championship meet in Houston, Texas. She won the championship in the heptathlon for a second year in a row and set a record.

5

GREAT EXPECTATIONS

WITH THE TURMOIL and major adjustments of her freshman year behind her, Joyner sailed into her sophomore year with all systems go. She chose history as her major and tackled the stiffer requirements of college academics with the same discipline and success she had brought to her high school studies. But she really came into her own in the sports arena.

She promptly met Kersee's expectations with her performance on the Bruins' track team. When the Bruins won the National Collegiate Athletic Association (NCAA) Track and Field Championship, she had scored 32 of the team's 153 winning points. In 1982, less than a year after taking on the heptathlon, she won the NCAA heptathlon championship and, never one to do things by halves, she set an NCAA record with a score of 6,099 points to become the top collegiate heptathlete.

Also in 1982, Joyner won the national championship in the heptathlon, held by the Athletics Congress, the U.S. governing body of track and field. That win meant that she was now ranked as the best heptathlete in the nation. She also competed in the long jump, which she barely missed winning, coming in a close second. For her combined prowess in basketball and track and field, she was named UCLA's All-University Athlete.

If freshman year had been a roller coaster of joy and sadness, sophomore year whizzed by, a whirl of achievements and hard work. And almost before Joyner noticed, she found herself in her junior year and still riding high.

Joyner had always pushed her brother Al to keep up with his sports, even when she had had to drag him out

Joyner (first row, second from left) poses with the 1982 UCLA Bruins. She was named UCLA All-University Athlete in basketball and track and field that year and also won the Athletic Congress's National Championship Award for the heptathlon.

of bed in the morning to practice. He never minded that she was two years younger and cheerfully followed his sister's lead.

Their mother's death had drawn them even closer to each other, and though they were at different colleges, they kept in touch, phoning each other often to exchange the latest news. Because they both were into track and field, they would sometimes find themselves at the same track meets, and they both felt this gave them a certain edge. Al has an explanation for their closeness; "We've got a special kind of ESP," he says.

To their mutual delight, they both made the U.S. team going to the World Championships in Helsinki, Finland, in the summer of 1983. Although the World Championships do not give medals, as the Olympics do, the winners are entitled to call themselves World Champions, and the competitions are held every four years, as are the Olympics.

By now they were both experienced competitors with strong records behind them, and they looked forward to this chance to show the world what they could do. But no matter how good an athlete's record, every competition is a new challenge and anything can happen. There are no sure things in sports events.

Al was a jumper. In his events, competitors get six chances to score. Only the best score counts, meaning the athlete has six chances to win. Unfortunately, Al pulled a hamstring during the triple-jump competition. This is a common injury, especially for track-and-field athletes, but it is at least temporarily disabling. Al tried to overcome it but he was able to place only eighth.

Jackie was competing in the heptathlon, which meant her event would consist of seven different sports played out over two days. The strenuous demands of the heptathlon on the muscles require that an athlete pay constant attention to them to keep them in shape. No one knew this better than Joyner, who by now was an experienced hep-

Al Joyner qualifies for the Olympic triple jump on August 3, 1984. The next day, he briefly left his event before the fourth round so he could see how his sister was doing and offer his support as she ran her final lap. By the end of the day, Al had won the gold medal in the triple jump and Jackie had won the silver in the heptathlon.

tathlete. She usually kept her muscles supple by applying ice to her legs between events, especially in the evening after the first day.

Somehow, distracted by one thing or another, she neglected this critical routine and went to bed without any preparation for the next day's demands. Predictably, she found in the morning that her legs were sore and aching, and when she tried to loosen them up during warm-ups, they did not respond as she had hoped and she pulled a hamstring muscle, just as her brother had done.

Al and Jackie returned to the United States, disappointed with their poor performances, but experienced enough to know that injuries happen even to the best athletes and, happily, there is always another competition in the wings to look forward to. This time it was the one they had both been dreaming of all their lives.

The next item on their mutual agenda was getting in shape for the 1984 Olympics, which would be held in Los Angeles the following summer. For them, preparation had become a family affair because Al and Jackie were both training at UCLA. Al had already completed his college eligibility at Arkansas State, but he was still competing full time, both nationally and internationally. He had been impressed with Kersee's growing reputation and his coaching of Jackie and had moved to Los Angeles to train with Kersee. Both he and his sister were now practicing at UCLA's Drake Stadium, just across the field from each other.

Joyner was especially fortunate to have Kersee for her coach. He was earning a reputation as one of the brightest young track-and-field coaches in the country and scores of young athletes were vying to train with him. An example of Kersee's technique and how thoroughly he prepared his training program for Jackie is the time when he had her evaluated by Bob Forster, a leading physical therapist practicing in Los Angeles. Kersee wanted Forster's professional opinion of Joyner's capabilities. His evaluation could not have been more enthusiastic. "She was like a gem in the raw. After examining her, though, I told him: 'This girl's the real thing.'"

That was all Kersee needed to hear to go ahead full steam. As Pat Jordon wrote in an October 1988 article in *Life* magazine, "His genius is in recognizing raw talent and channeling it in its natural direction." In Joyner he had found every coach's dream of a moldable world-class athlete who would take direction and had the ability to deliver. Not only did he guide her into the best showcase for her particular talents, he deliberately chose a new Olympic event for her, the heptathlon. He reasoned that she was a natural multiathlete, and that she was too good to waste her time mired in a sport that would lead nowhere once she graduated from college. The quality and foresight of his judgment is evident in the statistics from his 1983–84 year as track coach for the World Class Athletic Club in Long Beach, California. By the end of the 1984 Olympics, he had seven medalists at the Games.

With the Olympics just around the corner, Joyner went into overdrive. First, at Kersee's suggestion, she arranged to take the 1983–84 year off from basketball so she could concentrate on her Olympic sports. Permission to do this may be granted under the rules of the NCAA, which allows athletes to compete for four years in their scholarship sport but allots them five years in which to do it. The college agrees to permit such an athlete to retain her scholarship as long as she agrees to return the following year to complete her obligations.

Although she enjoyed basketball, putting it on temporary hold was a valuable concession. For the first time in her life, Joyner was free to relentlessly pursue her goal, and no laser beam was ever more sharply focused than her single-minded commitment to practicing and improving her performance. Her days were spent in an unvarying routine: first classes, then to the track field for long-jump and heptathlon practice. Regardless of the demands of her academic schedule, she managed to practice eight hours every day. As for her diet, she tried to eat balanced meals and to avoid junk foods.

An important part of her training was competition in just about every possible event that came along. For Joyner, that meant a steady round of competitions as well as practice. In 1983, she won the NCAA Broderick Award. That made official what the sports world had already recognized: she was designated the top female track-and-field athlete in the United States.

At the beginning of 1984, she entered the long-jump competition at the Bally Invitational Meet in Chicago, Illinois. In spite of her success with the heptathlon, the long jump was still Joyner's favorite sport. It was also a particularly satisfactory event for the winter indoor season and she enjoyed being able to concentrate more on it. She explained, "Jumping has always been the thing to me. It's like leaping for joy, but, of course, there's more to it than that. Your competitor has just done 21 feet, another competitor is on the runway, and I'm behind her. You have to respond here and now. It lets you know what you're made of." True to form, Joyner once again showed what she was made of; she did not just win, she set a new American indoor record of 21 feet 6½ inches.

Track and field has two seasons; it occurs indoors in the winter and outdoors in the spring and summer. Winter track and field usually is confined to sprints, hurdles, and the long jump because there is no indoor heptathlon. But Joyner was not about to let the weather interfere with her all-event practicing. Southern California winters do not have snow or really cold weather, so she would simply bundle up as much as necessary, and go outdoors for her javelin and shot put hours.

The javelin throw and shot putting were still her least favorite sports, and she had trouble achieving her usual high standards in these sports. To improve her performance, she worked on those parts of her body that were not built up to their maximum because they were not especially required in running and long jump. She lifted weights to build up her arm muscles and upper-body strength for throwing the javelin as far as possible, and handling the 8-pound-13-ounce weight of the shot put ball. In addition, she practiced the specific skills and techniques

Joyner competes in the 800-meter run during the NCAA Outdoor Track and Field Championships in Houston in June 1983. That same year Joyner won the Broderick Award as the top female track-and-field athlete in the United States.

A view from the stands of UCLA's Drake Stadium shows the steepness of the steps that Joyner had to run up and down during her training for the heptathlon. Coach Kersee knew how to push Joyner to the utmost to be the best, even when she complained about his demands.

peculiar to each of these unusual sports. She concentrated particularly on both the run-up for the javelin, which is crucial to the distance achieved in its throw, and on the body spin for the shot put, which generates the power for putting the shot a winning distance.

As her coach, Kersee helped her set her priorities. "It takes a lot of time, a lot of juggling, a lot of organization, and a lot of detail work trying to figure out which event to work on first, what each event should be focused on. And we just work day by day, week by week, trying to get all these little things down." The "little things" were a kind of fine tuning that Kersee was good at. Whereas Joyner was an intuitively good athlete, Kersee was adept at charting each practice session. Sometimes he would sit down and show her how to compare her scores in specific events with the scores of the winners and how to analyze them. She could then see for herself where she needed to improve. "Bob showed me on paper first," she says. She could see by the statistics that "Jane Frederick was beating me by 400 points in just two events, the shot put and the javelin." Because Frederick was currently the best American heptathlete, she was the one Joyner had to beat. She saw also that the advantage she was gaining because of her exceptional speed was overshadowed by her poor performance in the hurdles, so she targeted this event for special work.

Kersee was able to help Joyner develop better technique so that she maximized her speed and used the spring in her legs to sail over the hurdles instead of catching her foot on them. Even so apparently small a change as taking off on the proper foot made a big difference in her time.

Kersee gives his athletes everything he has but demands just as much in return. One time Joyner complained because he made her train by running up and down the hundreds of steps that compose the stands of the Drake Stadium at UCLA. Kersee knew the right button to push: "Do you want to win the gold medal or the silver medal? Do you want to be standing there listening to the East German national anthem?" It was no contest. Joyner wanted to win the gold and she wanted to hear the U.S. national anthem as she mounted the winning podium. She ran back up the steps.

Joyner works out at Parson's Field in East St. Louis before the 1984 Olympic Games. Her first step toward getting to the Olympics was making the U.S. Olympic heptathlon team; there were only three places on the team and she had to compete against 21 of the nation's best heptathletes.

6

THE DREAM COMES TRUE—ALMOST

THE 1984 OLYMPIC GAMES were in the wings, waiting to make their grand entrance before the whole world the coming summer, on July 28. But first the U.S. Olympic teams had to be chosen. From all over the country, the finest athletes converged on Los Angeles with high hopes and great expectations. Sportswriters were making their informed predictions but, as every experienced athlete knew, luck would play a part; an unexpected upset was always possible. Reputations, even entire careers, were about to be made or put on hold, depending on who made the Olympic teams; ability and past performance were no guarantee of success.

To make the U.S. Olympic Heptathlon Team, Joyner first had to compete in June in the national track meet event of the Olympic Trials. There are only three places on the U.S. Olympic Heptathlon Team and 21 of the nation's top heptathletes were competing for them. This was her most important competition to date and she felt ready for it.

All the other heptathletes had reason to expect that they also were Olympic caliber. Among them were Jodi Anderson, from Chicago, who had won the 1980 heptathlon trials; Cindy Greiner, from Eugene, Oregon; and Patsy Walker, from the University of Houston; each had equally outstanding records. Joyner felt that of them all, Jane Frederick, who held the American heptathlon record of 6,457 points, was her most serious competitor.

Frederick was 32 years old, beginning to push the age envelope for a woman heptathlete, so this was probably her last chance to reach the Olympics. She was highly motivated also by the fact that, despite her outstanding record, she was competing in the Games for the first time. If she was going to win an Olympic gold medal, then this Olympics would probably have to be the one.

The first event was the 100-meter hurdles heat. A heat is a qualifying round in a running event that produces the required number of runners for the final. Joyner won with a time of 13.61 seconds. Jodi Anderson, however, won the next heat slightly faster, giving her the point lead in scoring.

The next event was the shot put, which Patsy Walker, playing through a tight field, won. The next and, as it turned out, crucial event, was the high jump.

The minimum height a jumper must reach to continue in competition is 5 feet 10¾ inches. This was one of Frederick's best events and would not usually have been a problem, but she had suffered a leg injury earlier and her leg was still bothering her. Contrary to everyone's expectations, she not only failed to win, she failed to clear even the minimum height. And as quickly and unbelievably as that, she was out of the competition.

Joyner, who always empathized with other athletes, was truly upset over Frederick's mishap. It was one thing to beat her fair and square, but she did not enjoy benefiting from another's disaster. Still, when Joyner's turn came, she cleared 6 feet, and moved up to a hefty lead.

By the end of the first day, the top four remaining contenders were so close in scoring that it was impossible to predict the winners, but Joyner was still in first place.

She looked forward to the second day, which started with her favorite, the long jump. Greiner went first with a good competitive jump. Walker did even better, scoring a personal best. But Joyner joyfully took off in a burst of speed, stretched and held her long legs in a breathtaking jump, and set a new American heptathlon long-jump best. She had jumped a full foot and a half farther than anyone else.

Neither of the two events remaining, the javelin throw and the 800-meter run, were Joyner's strong points. Aware of that, she had been training extra hard in them. Moreover, she got a lift during her lunch break, when Frederick came over to encourage her and to urge her to break her record. "Go for it," Frederick said.

In the javelin throw, an unusual thing happened; all four competitors threw high scores that were personal bests. Joyner's score placed her only third, but she was still ahead on cumulative points, which were what would count in the end.

In the last event, the 800-meter run, she failed to win but came in closely behind the winning Walker.

When the smoke had cleared, the next U.S. Olympic Heptathlon Team—Joyner, Anderson, and Greiner—had earned their place in the sun. Joyner's total of 6,520 points not only gave her the Olympic Trials Heptathlon victory, it set a new American record. In addition, Joyner had qualified for the Olympic Long-Jump Team, and was the sportswriters' pick to win one, if not two, gold medals.

Once again a sporting event became a family affair. With Al having qualified for the Olympic Triple-Jump Team, he and Jackie would both be on the field at the same time. Perhaps they would each win a gold medal! Just as they had shared so many things through the years, they would be together on the Olympic field of their dreams.

Jackie's sisters, Debra (left) and Angela, were among the fans cheering for Jackie and Al at the 1984 Olympics in Los Angeles.

Everything was going along well when suddenly fate took a hand. During training, just two weeks before Opening Day, Joyner suffered a recurring injury, first sustained during the 1983 World Championship in Helsinki, Finland. She strained her left hamstring muscle.

It was not the sort of injury that would keep her from competing, but when hamstrings go unused for any length of time, they tend to stiffen up. So, combining rest with exercise meant walking a very fine line between warming up and overstraining. Nothing was going to stop her now, so she walked it.

Joyner's first Olympics were spectacular. The pomp and pageantry were everything she had ever imagined, and her fans and supporters were behind her all the way. Though from her point of view she won *only* a silver medal, it was an Olympic medal, something most athletes never come close to in a lifetime. Furthermore, she had

At the 1984 Olympics, U.S. teammates Jodi Anderson (left) and Jackie Joyner take the hurdles with West Germany's Sabine Braun (right) during the 100-meter hurdles preliminaries for the heptathlon.

come in a very close second, only a heartbeat away from earning the gold.

Bob Kersee was not the least bit disappointed. He later said Joyner just was not mentally ready to win a gold medal at that time. And Joyner could not be unhappy for long because she could not help taking pleasure in her brother's success.

Although Al Joyner had risked his own competition by leaving it early to come to Jackie's support, he had won the Olympic gold medal in the triple jump, the first American in 80 years to do so. Shortly after, when Jackie got her silver medal, she was crying as she stepped off the platform. Al thought she was upset at not winning the gold and he hugged her. But she smiled through her tears. "I'm not crying because I lost. I'm crying because you won," she said happily.

In addition, Al and Jackie Joyner were the first brother and sister to win Olympic medals in track and field on the same day. Sports records are made to be broken, but that footnote to sports history will never be erased.

The future was full of promise. It was time for Joyner to return to UCLA to complete her college work and rejoin the basketball team. "I enjoy playing basketball and I miss it," she had said, and now she was free to play once again.

Meanwhile, Jane Frederick had recovered from her injury and won back the American heptathlon record at a meet in France. She knew the record would not be hers for long because Joyner was coming on strong. "I always thought she would be the one to lead the next generation, and it had to do with the kind of person she was. She had a sense of purpose. With Kersee's direction, she really gave herself to all seven events." Frederick was a realist, and she gracefully conceded the future to Joyner.

The basketball season and Joyner's college career on the court ended as spectacularly as it had begun five years earlier. In her last season, she led the Bruins to a 20–10 record, and was named first-team All-Conference.

In East St. Louis, Al Joyner leads a motorcade of 1984 Olympic winners—his sister Jackie waves to hometown crowds in the car behind him. After the Olympics, Joyner returned to UCLA to complete her coursework and play basketball.

She graduated from UCLA with recognition as one of the nation's top student-athletes, having established a collegiate long-jump record and a collegiate heptathlon record. In addition, she was the fourth leading career rebounder, the sixth best career scorer, and tenth on UCLA's all-time assist list. Coach Moore summed up her basketball star's ability, "If Jackie had specialized in basketball, she would have made the Olympic team."

Kersee was now head coach of the women's track team. He and Joyner were more and more comfortable with each other. "We could talk about absolutely anything. And whatever acclaim came to me didn't bother him," Joyner revealed. She had found that some of the men she had dated had been bothered by her achievements and celebrity status.

For him, his relationship with Joyner was a revelation. He said it was the first relationship of his life that he believed might become permanent. "I never had that many female friends. Who can when you're coaching from 6 o'clock in the morning until 8 o'clock at night and watching videotapes until 10 and trying to go to sleep right after 'Nightline' goes off. One girlfriend I had told me, 'You

put in more time with your athletics than you do with me.'
I couldn't deny it."

In 1984, Joyner had begun to notice a difference in the
way Kersee treated her. He had been impressed by how
well she had handled her disappointment with the Olympics, and now they were spending even more time training
together.

With Joyner, he had it both ways. He could spend all the
time he wanted on his "athletics," without her even thinking of complaining, because so much of it was spent
coaching her or accompanying her to meets.

And on her part, she could concentrate on everything
that mattered to her. Partly that meant she could continue
to give time to her beloved long jump: She went on a
whirlwind trip to Europe, joining the international track-
and-field circuit, and leaving a trail of new successes in
her wake, including a new American outdoor long-jump
record of 23 feet 9 inches in Zurich, Switzerland.

When she returned to the United States at the end of
the summer, she prompty went on to Baton Rouge, Louisiana, to compete in the National Sports Festival at South-

*Children from East St. Louis
surround their hometown
celebrities Al and Jackie
Joyner, who returned for a
visit after their successes
at the 1984 Olympics. U.S.
heptathlete Jane Frederick
said of Jackie, "I always
thought she would be the one
to lead the next generation,
and it had to do with the kind
of person she was. She had a
sense of purpose."*

On July 28, 1985, Joyner edges out Jill Lancaster in the heptathlon at the National Sports Festival in Baton Rouge, Louisiana, winning the gold. This festival was the first, but not the last, in which Joyner won all seven of the heptathlon events.

ern University. This was an especially calculated move because the Olympic Festival (as it is now called) is held in non-Olympic years and is an important part of the agenda for any athlete who hopes to make the next U.S. Olympic Team.

Instead of tiring of this steady round of competitions, Joyner seemed energized. At the Festival she set a new U.S. first-day best of 3,942 points and won in each of the first four events. She then went on to win all three the next day. This was the first, but not the last, time she was to win all seven heptathlon events. She also set a new NCAA record with her 6,718 points, although a less than challenging javelin throw kept her from bettering Frederick's U.S. heptathlon record.

In 1985, there were no heptathlons scheduled until summer, and in nonheptathlon seasons, Joyner participated in whatever track and field events she could find no matter how far she had to travel to them. Predictably, she left behind a string of successes and records. She had added the triple jump to her repertoire and soon had jumped the best jump, with 43 feet 4 inches, by an American woman that year. And when she tried the 400-meter hurdles, she came up with the fourth fastest time—55.05 seconds—by an American women in sports history.

One evening Kersee suggested Joyner meet him at the beach, just to talk. It was not exactly a date and what they talked about was not exactly personal. He asked her to predict her heptathlon scores for the next NCAA championships. Joyner recalled she thought at the time he had something else on his mind. "Nothing came of it at the time, but I went home and looked in the mirror and said, 'I think he likes me.' "

As a regular participant in the NCAA outdoor championships at Austin, Texas, that May, she qualified for the finals in five different events and in spite of the fact that she was unaccustomed to the Texas heat, she obtained the highest individual score at the event.

Meanwhile she and Kersee began to date. Kersee had come to realize "what was wrong with me was trying to find a wife outside athletics and trying to convince her that this is a big part of my life, and not to get mad because I come home and have four or five athletes with me and ask what's to eat for all of us."

They decided to keep their dating a secret. Joyner did not want anyone on the track team to think she was getting special treatment. "It would have been easy for them to say that he showed favoritism toward me. I never wanted anyone to feel that anything was given to me. I felt I had worked for everything."

One warm summer night in 1985, between pitches at a Houston Astros baseball game, Bob Kersee turned to Joyner and said, "You know, we get along so well, we might as well get married." It was not the most romantic proposal a woman had ever received, but apparently it suited Joyner just fine. She said yes.

Jackie Joyner-Kersee throws the javelin in the heptathlon competition at the Athletics Championships in Rome, Italy, on September 1, 1987. She later won the gold medal in the competition.

7

THE BEST OF TIMES

THE WHIRLWIND PACE of her sports rounds, academic work, and private life left Joyner still slightly behind schedule at the end of the 1984–85 school year. She completed her sports commitment to the college, making UCLA's All-University Athlete for the third time, but she needed another half year of school to earn her degree. The college, not about to stand in the way of this overachiever, once again granted her time off. She took off the 1985–86 semesters, planning to return the following school year to earn the missing credits. But time out did not mean she *just* took the year off.

On January 11, 1986, Jackie Joyner and Bob Kersee were married in the small Saint Luke's Baptist Church in Long Beach, California, where Kersee was associate pastor.

It was a happy wedding with Al Joyner serving a double role—giving the bride away and supervising the photographs. And it got a little hectic. "When they asked, 'Who gives this woman?'" Al remembers, "I was out in the crowd showing Jeanette Bolden (a member of the 1984 Olympic gold medal relay team) how to work the camera. I said 'Agh! I do! And good luck.'"

The wedding couple almost cracked up trying to fit the wedding rings on each other, and the preacher said, "This is going to be a happy marriage."

Bob and Jackie are still happily married, and years after their wedding, Kersee summed up their success. "I think not being married to an athlete would be difficult because of the time I put in at the track. It would be a shame if we let track and field get in the way of our relationship, or if we let our relationship get in the way of track and field. We both have high goals. I'm happy that it works for both of us."

Their marriage works because they work at it. Kersee explains, "We want to make it in terms of what we've got to do athletically, and we want to stay married for the rest of our lives. So we've got rules in terms of our coach-athlete relationship and our husband-wife relationship. Jackie is easy to coach but she's opinionated, and I'm opinionated. I'm a yeller, I'm going to get my point across. I've been married 2½ years; I've been coaching for 17. So I know more about coaching than about being married. Jackie's an athlete of mine, and I'm not going to treat her any better or any worse than I treat any of my athletes."

They argue a lot but it does not affect their relationship. "Jackie and I have too many things to do to let these things linger," Kersee says. "We're going to play our games, but once it's over, we're going to sit down and think about it. If I'm wrong, I'm going to make some adjustments. If Jackie's wrong, she's not going to admit it, but she'll make some adjustments."

Joyner-Kersee laughingly agrees. "I *am* a bit stubborn. I guess I ought to be the one who says, 'I'm sorry, you were right.' But it's hard for me to say that. I'd rather make Bobby feel frustrated than tell him, 'I know you were right.' But at least we keep it on the athletic field. When we go home, it's as husband and wife. That means Bobby laying on the couch, asking me if I'll run him some bath water."

They agree on their roles both at home and at work, and this makes their relationship go more smoothly. Joyner-Kersee says Bob often does the cooking, which she hates to do, and his share of other chores, but he always has the deciding vote. He explains, "My philosophy is 49–49. Whenever I coach anybody, they have 49% of the say, and I have 49%. When it comes down to someone having to make a decision, I have the 2%. At home, it's 49–49. If I feel like doing the dishes, I do the dishes. If she has to do the dishes, she has to do the dishes. The 2% is always mine. Jackie wants at least half of the 2%. She's always negotiating for it, but she hasn't got it. I'm not Jackie's boss at home, but I have to have a leadership role. When an argument occurs, I have to know that I have 51%."

In 1986, Joyner-Kersee appeared on Joan River's "Late Show" TV program. She showed a surprised press and public another side of her personality, dressing up in a spectacular, bare-shouldered evening gown, and looking every inch the celebrity she was rapidly becoming.

Meanwhile exciting new things were happening in track and field. The first Goodwill Games were to be held in Moscow, Russia, in the summer of 1986. The Games were the brainchild of Ted Turner, a top communications executive. His idea was to bring together the many athletes from all over the world who had missed competing with each other because of the U.S. and Russian boycotts of the previous two Olympics. He was able to guarantee that the Goodwill Games would be televised throughout the world on his Cable News Network (CNN). Joyner-Kersee planned to compete but meanwhile she had a number of other events to attend.

On July 7, 1986, Bob Kersee tries to cool off his wife after she completed the women's 800-meter race in the heptathlon at the Goodwill Games in Moscow, Russia. Joyner broke the 7,000-point mark with a total of 7,148— the only American woman to hold a world record in a multievent since Babe Didrikson.

Joyner-Kersee had joined her husband's World Class Track Club, and had also acquired a sponsor, Adidas. She was now a celebrity and was in demand for television appearances and personal appearances around the country. Her fans grew in number and enthusiasm and she used her popularity to try to be a good role model and to help young athletes whenever she found the opportunity.

Joyner-Kersee's 1986 heptathlon season began with a warm-up event in April, at the Mount San Antonio College Relays in California. As usual, she would not settle for just a win; she scored a personal high of 6,910 points, enough to top Frederick's American record. Unfortunately, it did not count because during the 200-meter race, the automatic timer had broken.

She soon made up for it in Gotzis, Austria, in May at the Gotzis International track-and-field meet, where she again broke Frederick's heptathlon record, also defeating another top athlete, Anke Behmer of East Germany, with 6,841 points. Joyner-Kersee topped it off when she was given, for the second year in a row, the NCAA Broderick Cup award as the nation's top collegiate female athlete.

But her crowning achievement for the year came in July, when Joyner-Kersee and Bob Kersee went to Moscow for the Goodwill Games. At the beginning of their marriage, Kersee had said she could not use his name until she had set a world record. That demand posed no problem for her and this was her chance to prove it. On July 7, she swept the field the first day of the heptathlon, setting an American best in the 100-meter high hurdles with a time of 12.85 seconds, a personal best in the high jump with a distance of 6 feet 2 inches, and a personal best of 23 seconds in the 200-meter, beating the first-day world-best record that had been set in 1985 with her 4,151 points. She was way ahead in points of the previous two-day world record set in 1984.

The second day, when her competitors thought she might slow down after her incredible first-day wins, she really took off. Joyner-Kersee leapt a heptathlon world record in the long jump, and threw her best ever in the javelin. The last event to come was the grueling 800-meter race. Joyner-Kersee had set her heart on scoring 7,000 points.

Sportswriters had long argued whether a woman could ever score 7,000 points and the consensus was that it was impossible and would never happen. That day everyone knew Joyner-Kersee was going to try to do it and almost everyone believed it could not be done. Before the 800-meter run began, the announcer said over the loud speaker that she needed a time of 2:24.64 to break the 7,000-point barrier.

With the cheering crowd going wild in the stands, she did even better: she finished in 2:10.02, giving her a total score of 7,148 points, 202 points over the old record. She got a standing ovation and the excited announcer said, in Russian and in English, "It's marvelous. It's magnificent!"

She was now the first American woman to hold the world record in a multievent since her idol Babe Didrikson had set her own record in the triathlon more than 50 years earlier.

Joyner-Kersee did not gloat. She told the reporters, who had doubted her ability, "I feel very blessed today to come here and do this. I feel that I've paid my dues. I knew good things would come my way because I have been very humble and patient waiting for this to happen."

But the sportswriters did not give up easily. They were not about to admit they had been wrong. Dwight Stones, a high jumper turned TV commentator, said to her, "No way you're ever going to do *that* again." But, as he was to shortly discover, he was looking in a clouded crystal ball.

Joyner-Kersee next competed in the U.S. Olympic Sports Festival in Houston, Texas, held in August 1986.

Joyner-Kersee clears the bar of the high-jump portion of the heptathlon competition at the U.S. Olympic Festival in Houston, Texas, on August 1, 1986. She broke her own new record, scoring 7,158 points in the heptathlon.

The temperature was 126 degrees Fahrenheit, the first hot August day of the heptathlon, and at the day's end, Joyner-Kersee gave a press conference sitting on two bags of ice. In spite of the heat, she set world bests and personal bests as if they were routine, and confounded the naysayers by breaking her own new record, scoring 7,158 points. Even Kersee was impressed. "To do it again in this short period of time is truly amazing," he said.

She broke her own record for honors in 1987. Joyner-Kersee received the Jesse Owens Memorial Award, was named Women's Athlete of the Year by *Track & Field News* magazine, Sportswoman of the Year by the U.S. Olympic Committee, and became only the eighth woman in 67 years to win the Sullivan Award, given by the Amateur Athletics Union to the nation's outstanding amateur athlete. For the Sullivan Award, she had to compete with U.S. Naval Academy basketball star David Robinson and University of Miami quarterback Vinny Testaverde.

Al Joyner, reflecting on her win over Testaverde, said, "She beat out a Heisman Trophy winner. That's something I can tell my grandchildren about. She wasn't just the best woman athlete in America. They voted her the best American athlete, period."

Mission accomplished for the time being, Joyner-Kersee went back to college. She earned her degree as a history major in December, and she and her husband bought a house in Long Beach, California. They commuted daily to work at the UCLA campus: Kersee as the UCLA women's track team head coach and Joyner-Kersee to continue her training as one of his athletes.

Meanwhile, the focus zeroed in on the 1988 Olympic Games in Seoul, South Korea.

Getting ready for the Olympics is not a simple onetime task. One of the best ways to train is to enter as many competitions, especially heptathlon events, as possible. The key event in 1987 was the World Championships in Rome, Italy, which was to occur that summer. Joyner-

On April 4, 1987, Joyner-Kersee accepts the 1986 Sportswoman of the Year trophy, presented by the U.S. Olympic Committee, at a banquet in Indianapolis, Indiana.

On February 23, 1987, Joyner-Kersee accepts the 1986 James E. Sullivan Memorial Award from the 1985 winner, marathoner Joan Benoit-Samuelson. Al Joyner remarked that now he had something he could tell his grandchildren about: "[Jackie] wasn't just the best woman athlete in America. They voted her the best American athlete, period."

Kersee set her goals for the worlds. Winning was a given, but more than that she hoped to once again break her own record. She was aiming at 7,200 points.

Together, the coach and the athlete analyzed their strategy. "Of course goal number one is to be prepared in the worlds in Rome in September. For that, the 800 is the key. If she's prepared in the 800, she'll be double ready for the other events," said Kersee.

In the meantime, in serious training, Joyner-Kersee participated in the Mobil Indoor Track and Field Grand Prix for an overall indoor champion title where she was named the meet's Outstanding Athlete. Next, in May 1987, she entered the Pepsi Invitational at UCLA, and promptly set records in the long jump (21 feet 10 inches) and 100-meter hurdles (7.45 seconds). However, her javelin technique still required work if it was not to lower her overall score.

Over Kersee's objections that it was only two weeks before the worlds, Joyner-Kersee insisted on competing in the Pan-American Games in Indianapolis, Indiana, in August 1987. Through a twist of fate, this turned out to be an important decision.

At the Pan-American Games, a fan asked her to autograph her picture in a magazine. It was next to a picture of jumper Heike Drechsler of East Germany. It showed Drechsler airborne in her long jump, with her legs fully extended, exactly the position Kersee had been urging on Joyner-Kersee.

Days later, Joyner-Kersee emulated the technique and completed her long jump tying Drechsler's world record of 24 feet 5½ inches. Joyner was now the only American woman to simultaneously hold a world record in both a multievent and a single event.

Though she was understandably elated, Kersee's reaction was even stronger. He dropped to his knees and, surrounded by reporters, he could not stop crying. "I'm so emotional because we were so close to not coming here. I have to ask myself: Am I so overprotective that I could have kept her from this?" Joyner-Kersee went over and hugged him. "So now I can long-jump, huh?" she joked.

Time does not stand still for a champion and by the end of August, the Kersees were in Rome, Italy, for the worlds. Joyner-Kersee had the highest first-day total on record at the end of the first day. But the heat and humidity got to her the second day; she had a headache and she was dehydrated. She felt better a few days later, when she faced the long jump with her co-world-record holder, Drechsler.

Drechsler, however, was hampered by an injury she had been hiding. After her first jump, the knee was so painful she had to withdraw and concede the gold medal to Joyner-Kersee. Drechsler and Joyner-Kersee hugged each other. They had shared the experience of numerous

In June 1987, Joyner-Kersee listens to her coach-husband critique her poor performance in the javelin, which prevented her from a world record in the heptathlon during the USA-Mobil Outdoor Track and Field Championships in San Jose, California. She nevertheless produced the third-highest point total in heptathlon history, with 6,979 points.

On August 13, 1987, Joyner-Kersee makes her second jump in the long jump at the Pan American Games. On her sixth attempt, she tied the world record with a jump of 24 feet 5 1/2 inches.

sports injuries, and they knew it was just something that happened. Kersee calls them "the Ali and Frazier of the women's long jump. You know they'll force the best out of each other. And no matter who wins, you know it won't change their feelings for one another."

Meanwhile, what the press was calling "The First Family of Track," gained a new member. Al Joyner became engaged to marry Florence Griffith. Griffith had been on the UCLA women's track team and had been one of Kersee's athletes. She was a track-and-field champion who had won a silver medal in the 1984 Olympics, and both silver and gold medals in the 1987 worlds. When she and Al Joyner became engaged, she gave him the gold medal. The couple got married in October 1987.

Temperamentally, Florence Griffith Joyner and Jackie Joyner-Kersee are very different. Florence likes attention and dresses flamboyantly. At the 1988 Olympics, she painted her long fingernails a different color each day, and her running outfit for the 200-meter dash was a pair of white bikini bottoms and white lace leotards. When Jackie was asked why she does not wear sexy bodysuits, she said, "Oh, it's nice, but it's not me. I couldn't concentrate on what I was doing. I'd be listening to the people in the stands laughing at me." Before an event, she prefers to sit quietly with Kersee, away from the press, discussing strategy.

Joyner-Kersee's attitude harks back to her mother's upbringing. "I was brought up to wear long dresses. Never to be flashy. My mother used to dress me from the fifties when I was a teenager. She was only a child herself, raising a child, and she wanted to protect me. I couldn't date boys until I was eighteen. So I just lost myself in school and sports."

In spite of her mother's strictness, there was always a great deal of love, and Joyner-Kersee grew up knowing how to make the best of whatever came her way. Coach Moore characterized her when Joyner-Kersee was at UCLA, saying "She thoroughly enjoys everything she's doing. She makes everything feel special. That's her natural way. She could be carrying the heaviest burden in the world and she'd still be smiling."

In some ways the heaviest burden Joyner-Kersee carries is her asthma. She has been hospitalized several times, and her lifestyle makes it impossible to follow the regimen that would keep it under control. For instance, there are drugs that asthmatics can use, both to prevent attacks and to minimize them when they occur. But they all contain ingredients that are banned by the International Olympic Committee, and the fact that they are prescribed by a physician for a specific illness, does not make a difference. She cannot use the drugs the Committee does allow because they would affect her coordination and make her sleepy. Joyner-Kersee's reaction is pure frustration, "I can control so much of what I do and I can't control this asthma. Sometimes I don't want to accept that I have asthma." And lots of times she does not. She does not like to admit she is having an attack, even though sometimes it scares her. "I can't handle an attack, I panic," she says.

Kersee tries to watch out for her. One time he found her gasping for breath, doubled over in an effort to get air into her lungs. He and Al tried to persuade her to go to the hospital—they finally got her into the car and took off for the emergency room. When they got to the hospital, she did not want to go in, because she was sure that she could still get the attack under control. Kersee saw there was no point in arguing. "I just picked her up and carried her through the door," he said. That attack was so severe that she spent two days in the hospital.

But Joyner-Kersee had set her sights on the 1988 Olympic Games to be held in Seoul, Korea, in September. *Nothing* was going to stop her now.

At the 1992 Olympics in Barcelona, Germany's Heike Drechsler shows her form in the long jump. Bob Kersee wanted Jackie to use Drechsler's technique, with fully extended legs, in her long jump at the 1987 Pan American Games. Joyner-Kersee tried the position and tied Drechsler's world record.

On September 29, 1988, Jackie and Bob Kersee hold an American sign during the Olympics in Seoul, South Korea. Jackie broke the Olympic records in the long jump, both in the separate event, with her 24-feet-3$\frac{1}{2}$-inch distance, and in the long-jump portion of the heptathlon, with 23 feet 10$\frac{1}{4}$ inches.

8

AS GOOD AS IT GETS

IN THE SUMMER OF 1988, both Joyner-Kersee and her sister-in-law, Griffith Joyner, tried out at the U.S. Olympic Trials in Indianapolis. They turned in a stellar performance with their respective events. In the 100-meter dash, Griffith Joyner finished first, setting a new world record, and won the 200-meter race, just shy of the world mark. Joyner-Kersee, competing in 103-degrees-Fahrenheit heat, broke three heptathlon records, scored her second-best shot put ever in a sudden rainstorm, and ended with a first-day record number of points.

The second day of the Trials, Joyner-Kersee won, beating her own world heptathlon record. As U.S. heptathlete Cindy Greiner put it, "Jackie does her thing and the rest of us compete for runner up." The third day, in the long jump, she won back the world outdoor record she had lost to Galina Chistyakova of the Soviet Union in June 1988.

Later that day, one of the trainers brought in a rubbing table so that Joyner-Kersee could lie down on bags of ice for a massage as she answered reporters' questions. She was happy with her performance so far, and cheerfully submitted to the roomful of television cameramen and reporters.

While she was talking, the public address system began to report the names of the athletes who had qualified for the 1988 U.S. Olympic Triple-Jump Team. Joyner-Kersee stopped in midsentence, listening for her brother's

In July 1988, Joyner-Kersee long jumps during the heptathlon competition at the U.S. Olympic Track and Field Trials in Indianapolis, Indiana, where she set a world record with 7,215 points. Soon after her performance, however, she received the news that her brother had not qualified for the triple-jump team.

name. As the first and second of the three names were read, she closed her eyes and clenched her fists. But the third name was not "Al Joyner." Jackie put her head on the table and cried. And when she tried to stop, she only cried more.

Al was disappointed but he joked about it. "She cried when I won in L.A.," he said, "and now she's cried when I lost."

That fall, halfway around the world, the city of Seoul, Korea, was gearing up for the 1988 Olympic Games. Al Joyner was on the plane with the U.S. Olympic Track and Field team. Even though he had not made the team, his wife and his sister had, and he put aside his own disappointment to give his support to the family. "I've got to go now. I got my gold medal in 1984, but my sister and my wife got silvers. I've got to help them get golds."

Joyner-Kersee hugs fellow heptathlete Terri Turner after Joyner-Kersee set a new U.S. record of 6 feet 4 inches for the high jump on July 15, 1988. Earlier at the trials she had set a record in the 100-meter hurdles.

On September 23, 1988, Joyner-Kersee clears the 100-meter hurdles in the heptathlon competition at the Olympics in Seoul. After winning the hurdles event with a time of 12.69 seconds, she went on to the high jump, during which she twisted her knee.

Joyner-Kersee had come a long way from the heartbreak of 1984. Now she was "the world record holder, heptathlon world champion, leading world athlete," and she was determined that this time she would win her gold medal.

Almost everyone in the sports world was rooting for her. After all, she had not lost a heptathlon since the 1984 Olympic Games and she had already done what most people believed was the impossible. She had proved, not once but *three* times, that a woman athlete could top a heptathlon score of 7,000 points. In addition, she was hired as a spokesperson for the beverage 7-Up and won her second Annual *Essence* Award.

On the airplane trip to Seoul, Joyner-Kersee needed to rest, but, although the flight to Seoul took 12 hours, she was too excited to sleep. "Now that I'm on the plane going to Seoul, I'm really starting to feel it."

At the Games, which were held from September 17 to September 24, the heptathlon event started badly. After winning the 100-meter hurdles in 12.69 seconds, she twisted her knee in the high jump but gritted her teeth and pushed on. The shot put score was good, 15.8 meters, and she won the 200-meter race, finishing the first day in first place.

She ignored the continuing pain of her injured knee and set the long-jump record the second day of the heptathlon with 23 feet 10¼ inches. By the end of the last event, the 800-meter race, she had run 2.08.51 minutes and set a new world heptathlon record with 7,291 points, winning her gold medal in true Joyner-Kersee style.

Just five days later, she competed in the long jump against Chistyakova, the world record holder, and Drechsler, her friendly rival. After four jumps with still no clear winner, Joyner-Kersee came up for her fifth jump. She took off as if she had wings on her heels, and soared through the air to a new Olympic record of 24 feet 3½ inches, the first American woman ever to win the Olympic long jump, and the first American woman, since Mildred L. McDaniel won the high jump in 1956, to win a field event. She had won not only one gold medal but two!

Just to make everything perfect, Griffith Joyner had won three gold medals, one for the 100-meter run (10.54 seconds), another for the 200-meter run (21.34 seconds), and a third with the 4 x 100 relay team (41.98 seconds).

But there were storm clouds on the horizon. It began with the disclosure that a Canadian sprinter, Ben Johnson, was found to have used steroids in his training. Steroids can have dangerous side effects and may cause cancer, but some athletes feel they will be able to train harder if they use them. Their use is strictly forbidden by the Olympic Committee; any athlete found to have used them may be suspended from competition for a period from three

Joyner-Kersee tosses the shot for a distance of 15.8 meters (51.4 feet) at the 1988 Olympics. The regulation weight of a shot for women in the Olympics is 8 pounds 13 ounces.

months to life, and even be stripped of any medals he or she may have won.

Once accusations started to fly, Joaquim Cruz of Brazil's Olympic team suddenly accused Joyner-Kersee and Griffith Joyner of using anabolic steroids. Asked how he knew the athletes were taking the drugs, he said he could tell by their appearance. "Florence, in 1984, you could see an extremely feminine person, but today she looks more like a man than a woman. . . . So these people must be doing something which isn't normal to gain all these muscles." Fortunately, the Olympic Committee routinely conducts random drug tests; they dismissed Cruz's charges, saying that these tests showed no traces of banned substances.

Joyner-Kersee, who does not even take the asthma drugs she needs, said, "I'm sad and sorry that people are implying that I'm doing something, because I've worked hard to get where I am today. There are a lot of reasons now why I won't even take a drink. I don't feel like putting

In February 1989, Bob Kersee kisses his wife after she received the trophy for being named the outstanding performer at the 1989 Millrose Games. Joyner-Kersee tied the world indoor record in the 55-meter hurdles at New York's Madison Square Garden with her time of 7.37 seconds.

anything into my body. It took a long time before I would even take an aspirin."

Cruz backed down. He denied he had ever made such an accusation, and the incident was soon forgotten.

In 1989, there were no big international heptathlons scheduled and Joyner-Kersee filled the gap by taking up hurdling. "I enjoy the sport," she said. "And I want to work toward new goals. I'm not just after Olympic titles and world records, I want to continue to excel."

And excel she did. During the indoor hurdling season, she tied the American record in 55-meter hurdles, beat the U.S. record in 60-meter hurdles, and won six straight 55-meter hurdles races at the Mobil/USA Indoor Track and Field Championships at New York's Madison Square Garden. At the end of the indoor season she was overall points leader on the Mobil Grand Prix tour. She and Kersee also added the 400-meter hurdles to her repertoire to increase her speed, endurance, and hurdling for the heptathlon races. "Training for one event keeps me strong in three," she said. "But I'm also taking this very seriously for its own sake." And in May 1989 she won the 400-meter hurdles at the Bruce Jenner Bud Light Classics in San Jose, California, in 57.15 seconds.

But in the middle of 1989, Joyner-Kersee began to show signs of strain. Her doctor said she was exhausted and needed a real rest to avoid having a complete breakdown. So a light schedule was planned for the 1990 indoor season. The strategy worked, and she won the Goodwill Games the following August. But she had pulled a leg muscle and was unable to compete for the rest of the year.

It was just as well; she had not recovered her health as much as she thought, and in November 1991 she suffered another severe asthma attack. She also came down with pneumonia, a disease especially dangerous for asthmatics because it affects the lungs.

The sports world began writing her off. Reporters asked what she was planning to do when she retired. But Kersee

Joyner-Kersee clears the 400-meter hurdles in the first-ever Jackie Joyner-Kersee Invitational track meet at UCLA's Drake Stadium in June 1989. She posted a time of 55.3 seconds, which was 1.85 seconds faster than the time she had posted two weeks earlier at the Bruce Jenner Bud Light Classics competition.

was optimistic about his wife regaining her health, and maybe switching to other track-and-field events. "If she ever worked on the long jump as hard as she works on the heptathlon, she says she could long-jump 25 feet and I believe her. If she concentrated on a single event, Lord knows what she's capable of doing."

Joyner-Kersee was on the same wavelength. Soon she began training for the National Championships in New York City. The winners of the National Championships would make the U.S. team that would compete in the World Championships to be held in Tokyo in August 1991. She was not at her best and the second day she suffered a groin injury, but went on to qualify for the team in both the heptathlon and the long jump.

As always, a win is history as soon as it happens, and an athlete's focus is already on the next challenge. The

World Championships in Tokyo were just a year before the 1992 Olympics in Barcelona, Spain. Joyner-Kersee wanted her performance at Tokyo to be one to show everyone that she was back in shape. But fate willed otherwise.

At the World Championships in Tokyo, the Soviet Union had increased its lead in the number of medals won in the track-and-field championships, and the United States was counting on Joyner-Kersee to help right the balance. In the long jump, her spiked shoe caught in the plasticene beyond the board, sharply twisting her right ankle. She fell hard and lay there, terrified that she had broken her leg and that she was looking at the end of her career. It turned out to be a strained hamstring muscle. She had it taped, and went on to win a gold, beating her friend and longtime rival Heike Drechsler.

The strain of the seven events of the heptathlon proved too much for Joyner-Kersee's leg. In the 200-meter sprint, she pulled up, hopped along for several meters and finally, her face clearly showing her pain, collapsed to the track in agony. As injuries go, it was not serious, but she had to retire from the heptathlon competition, and was forced to lay low for more than a month.

The following year, at the 1992 Olympics in Barcelona, Joyner-Kersee confounded those who thought she was through. Bob Kersee, a firm believer in the effect of attitude on winning, took Joyner-Kersee to a bullfight the Sunday before her events. He told her she had to approach her event like the matador and go in for the kill. "Only thing I don't want you doing, is cutting off their ears after they're dead," he said, referring to the usual custom. But Joyner-Kersee hated the bullfight and cheered for the bulls. And she firmly rejected Bob's comparison. "I don't need to act mean," she said, "not if I do what I'm capable of." And, as usual, her confidence was not misplaced. She won her third Olympic heptathlon for another gold medal with 7,044 points, the sixth time she had topped 7,000 points, retrieving the world record. She picked up a second gold in the long jump with a distance of 23 feet 3½ inches. Bruce Jenner, the 1976 decathlon champion, said that Joyner-Kersee had proved to the world that she was "the greatest multievent athlete ever, man or woman."

Further recognition came from Washington University in St. Louis, Missouri, when the university conferred on her an honorary Doctor of Law degree.

On March 5, 1994, at the USA/Mobil National Indoor Track and Field Championships held in Atlanta, Georgia, she sailed 23 feet 4¾ inches on her second round in the long jump and broke her 1992 American record of 23 feet 1¼ inches. Two and one-half hours later she ran the 60-meter hurdles and hit the fourth hurdle hard, almost breaking her left foot. After receiving X rays, she was told her foot was not broken, just badly bruised. "I tried to accelerate with Michelle [Freeman], " she said. "I forgot the hurdle was there. I don't know what happened. I know my ankle hurts. I've never really fallen hard like that. I thought I'd hit one of the girls, but then I found out I hit the hurdle."

Sometimes Kersee wants her to forget records and just set a slow, steady pace. In May 1994, shortly before the New York Games, Joyner-Kersee agreed to do exactly that. But when May 22 came, she won the long jump, sailing 24 feet 7 inches, breaking her 1987 American record, missing the 1988 world record by 1¼ inches. She got so enthusiastic about her jump that she decided against making a second one. "I was so excited. I was wheezing," Joyner-Kersee explained, "I thought, I don't want to have an asthma attack out here." The weather conditions that day at Columbia University's Wien Stadium, where the Games were being held, were almost perfect—it was warm and there was a little tailwind. At the time, Jackie's jump was the second longest jump in history by a woman, and the best jump ever on American soil. She attributed her success to her modified training regimen. "This year, my training has been about speed," she said. "We've been concentrating on the hurdles and the long jump, not the shot put or the javelin as in the past." Kersee elaborated by saying, "She was mad at me all indoor season, but today proves that the teacher is always smarter than the student." Further proof of Kersee's good judgment came during the Chemical Bank Millrose Games in New York City, where she won the high jump and 60-meter hurdles.

On July 26, 1994, while competing at the Goodwill Games in St. Petersburg, Russia, Joyner-Kersee was almost disqualified in the sixth round of the heptathlon because of a sticky javelin. A Russian referee accused her of putting a gluelike substance on her javelin to enable her to grip it better. Joyner-Kersee said the substance on her javelin was beer, which a fan had spilled on her equipment while it was in the stands. She had weighed in her javelins realizing they were wet from the beer, told her competitors that they were wet and then made practice throws with another athlete's javelins. The rules of the Games allow a competitor to use any of the javelins in the pool after each has been weighed and inspected by the judges. She said the Russian judges had approved hers and she put them in the pool but chose to use another competitor's javelin. After her third throw, however, a referee told her that she had broken the rules for using a substance to help with her grip, and she was disqualified. Jane Frederick called the charge an attempt to upset Joyner-Kersee's concentration for the event. By the time the event was to begin, Joyner-Kersee was notified that she had not been disqualified, but rather that she had been given a warning. Kersee believed the Russian referee owed his wife an apology and said, "You just don't do that to a world champion and three-time Goodwill Games winner."

In the javelin event, Joyner-Kersee finished fifth out of a field of eight, and last in the final event, the 800-meter

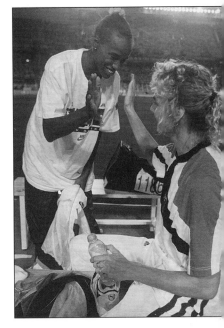

Joyner-Kersee gives Germany's Heike Drechsler a high five after the women's long-jump final at the 1992 Olympics in Barcelona, Spain. Drechsler won the gold in the event and Joyner-Kersee won the bronze.

Jackie Joyner-Kersee shows the gold medal she won in the heptathlon with a point total of 7,044 at the 1992 Olympics. "I just wanted to be an Olympian," Joyner-Kersee replied about her success. "It's been a blessing because I keep in mind how I got it. Not to take anything for granted. It all stuns me at times."

race, during which she had an asthma attack. Nevertheless, her total points, 6,606, gave her the lead—and the gold medal.

Clearly on a roll, in Brussels, Belgium, she competed in the IVO Van Damme Memorial where she won the long jump event with a distance of 24 feet. At the IAAF Mobil Grand Prix Final held in Paris, France, in September 1994, Joyner-Kersee tried to bounce back from a few injuries, including a strained right hamstring. She overcame her pain and went on to secure the women's title for the long jump with a 23-foot-8-inch leap. "I think this fills a gap in my career, Joyner-Kersee replied, "this is really a great end to my season."

Kersee says his wife is very competitive. Joyner-Kersee confesses that something just happens to her when someone sets a record in one of her events. "It just makes me hungrier," she says. She ascribes her success to her mother's upbringing. If Mary Joyner had not been so strict, and had not so carefully kept her from the hopelessness that pervaded her neighborhood, she might have settled for the life there. Perhaps if she had had to make do with fewer mayonnaise sandwiches instead of dinner, she might not have worked so hard to succeed.

"I just wanted to be an Olympian. In my dreams I never envisioned people asking for my autograph, going to the White House, being able to travel the world, meeting different people. Or being able to have a house or car or whatever. I never thought I would be like that. It's been a blessing because I keep in mind how I got it. Not to take anything for granted. It all stuns me at times."

Today, Joyner-Kersee is excelling in a totally different area. She is a successful and wealthy businesswoman, with endorsements and marketing contracts in which she promotes products as diverse as soft drinks and sunglasses, cheeseburgers and computers. She shares her good fortune through the Jackie Joyner-Kersee Community Foundation, which she established in 1988 in East St. Louis to raise money for sports, cultural, and educational programs for inner city youngsters.

Sometimes her outside activities cut into the time she spends on sports, but this does not worry her coach/husband. "She's much more of a fanatic about athletics than I am. I think that's saying something because before I met Jackie, I didn't think anyone could have more of a one-track mind than Bob Kersee."

One of her first beneficiaries was a recreation center in East St. Louis, Illinois, like the one that meant so much to her and Al when they were children. In addition, she raises money for her projects through personal appearances and speeches, and gives generously of her time and advice to other athletes who seek her out when they have a problem. She reaches out to children, granting scholarships through her Foundation, giving motivational talks sponsored by McDonald's in school assemblies, and visiting hospitals, churches, and schools in communities throughout the nation. "I like kids to get to know me. Sure, I've achieved a lot, but the thing is to let them see that everyone is raw material. I want to be a good statement of the possibilities."

At present, in preparation for the day she leaves the heptathlon, she is trying out other sports. "I've tried golf and I've learned that it's a lot harder than it looks, but it is something I want to do a lot of after Atlanta [the site of the 1996 Olympics]." She has never scored below 100, she says, but at times she is long and straight off the tee. There is also tennis and bowling, but all "after Atlanta." That is in the future—she is still very much a competitive world champion athlete. "Wouldn't it be great," she says, "to complete my career back on American soil, in Atlanta in 1996?"

She personally manages her foundation and charities from her home in Long Beach, California. She knows there will always be children and young athletes who need her help, and she simply says, "I believe it is the responsibility of Olympic champions to give something back to youth, to the public. It's our duty."

FURTHER READING

Biracree, Tom. *Wilma Rudolph.* New York: Chelsea House, 1988.

Guttman, Allen. *The Olympians. A History of the Modern Olympic Games.* Urbana: University of Illinois Press, 1992.

———. *Women's Sports: A History.* New York: Columbia University Press, 1991.

Henry, Bill, and Patricia Henry Yeomans. *An Approved History of the Olympic Games.* Los Angeles: Southern California Committee for the Olympic Games, 1984.

Lynn, Elizabeth A. *Babe Didrikson Zaharias: Champion Athlete.* New York: Chelsea House, 1989.

Page, James A. *Black Olympian Medalists.* Englewood, NJ: Libraries Unlimited, 1991.

Woolum, Janet. *Outstanding Women Athletes. Who They Are and How They Influenced Sports in America.* Phoenix, AR: Oryx Press, 1992.

CHRONOLOGY

1962   Born Jacqueline Joyner on March 3 in East St. Louis, Illinois

1971   Enters track-and-field, basketball, and volleyball programs at Mary E. Brown Community Center

1976   Wins National Championship in the pentathlon at the Junior Olympics

1977   Wins Junior Olympics National Championship in pentathlon for second year in a row; is featured in "Faces in the Crowd" section of *Sports Illustrated* magazine; enrolls in 10th grade at Lincoln High School in East St. Louis, where she joins track-and-field, basketball, and volleyball teams

1978   Sets state high school long-jump record; is named All-State and All-American in both track and basketball; wins Junior Olympics National Championship in pentathlon for the third year in a row

1979   Becomes captain of the track, volleyball, and basketball teams; basketball team wins state championship; the track team also wins the state title; Joyner wins the Junior Olympics National Championship in the pentathlon for the fourth year in a row

1980   Joyner enrolls at UCLA with a basketball scholarship; the Olympic Games in Moscow are boycotted by the United States because of the Soviet Union's military invasion of Afghanistan; Joyner is diagnosed as having asthma

1981   UCLA coach Bob Kersee coaches Joyner in the heptathlon; Mary Joyner, Jackie's mother, dies in January at age 38; Joyner wins the Broderick Award as the nation's top collegiate athlete

1982   In her sophomore year at UCLA, she wins the National Collegiate Athletic Association (NCAA) Championship Award given to the top college heptathlete; wins the National Championship Award given by the Athletics Congress, the governing body of track and field in the United States, to the best heptathlete in the country; sets new NCAA record as track team wins NCAA Championship; named UCLA All-University Athlete in basketball and track and field

1983   Named Most Valuable Player on the UCLA Bruins basketball team; wins NCAA championship in heptathlon for second time, setting a record; named Most Valuable Player of the UCLA women's track team; named All-University Athlete in basketball and track and field for the second time; wins Broderick Award again as nation's top collegiate track athlete; makes U.S. team competing in track-and-field World Championships in Helsinki, Finland

1984   Sets new American indoor record in long jump at Bally Invitational Meet, Chicago, Illinois; at the Olympic Trials in Los Angeles, Joyner wins heptathlon, setting a new American record, and wins the long-jump event; at the XXIII Olympics in Los Angeles, she wins the silver medal in the heptathlon

1985   Wins a third honor as UCLA's All-University Athlete; wins the Broderick Cup as the nation's outstanding collegiate sportswoman; at the National Sports Festival (today called the Olympic Festival) at Southern University in Baton Rouge, Louisiana, Joyner wins all seven events of the heptathlon for the first time

1986   Marries Coach Bob Kersee on January 11; she joins Kersee's World Class Track Club; Adidas sponsors her in its advertising; at the Goodwill Games in Moscow, she breaks the world record in the heptathlon with 7,148 points, the first woman to do so; at the U.S. Olympic Sports Festival in Houston, Texas, she again scores more than 7,000 for the second time, topping her own record, and says it is her "most memorable moment" in sports; she is named Athlete of the Year by *Track and Field News*; she wins the Jesse Owens Memorial Award as the Top Track and Field Athlete; she is awarded the Sullivan Award, given annually by the Amateur Athletes Union to the nation's outstanding amateur athlete; she appears on Joan Rivers's "Late Show" TV program; graduates from UCLA with a B.A. in history

1987   At the Pan-American Games, held in Indianapolis, Indiana, Joyner-Kersee wins the heptathlon and ties the world long-jump record of 24 feet 5½ inches, becoming the only American woman ever to hold a world record in a multievent and a single event at the same time; in Rome, Italy, at the World Track and Field Championships, Joyner-Kersee wins gold medals in the heptathlon and the long jump, becoming the first person since 1924 to capture gold medals in multisport and individual events at a world class competition; she is named Amateur Sportswoman of the Year by the Women's Sports Foundation; she wins a second consecutive Jesse Owens Award as best U.S. Track and Field Athlete; she receives the Associated Press Female Athlete of the Year Award; at the National Outdoor Championships, in San Jose, California, she wins both the National Heptathlon title, with the third highest point total—6,979—of all time, and the long jump, with the longest legal jump (23 feet 4½ inches) that year by a woman in the United States

1988   At the U.S. Olympic Trials in Indianapolis, she wins the heptathlon, setting a new world record of scoring more than 7,000 points for the fourth time; she scores a heptathlon personal record in the 100-meter hurdles, in the high jump, and in the 200-meter race; at the XXIV Olympics, in Seoul, South Korea, Joyner-Kersee wins the gold medal in the heptathlon and sets a new world record of 7,291 points; she wins a second gold medal and sets an Olympic record of 24 feet 3½ inches in the long jump, and she breaks a new world record in the 800-meter run; establishes the Jackie Joyner-Kersee Community Foundation in East St. Louis, Illinois, to raise money for sports, cultural, and education programs for inner-city youngsters; is hired as spokesperson for the beverage 7-Up; wins the second annual *Essence* Award

1989   Wins the 400-meter hurdle race in 57.15 seconds at the Bruce Jenner Bud Light Classics in San Jose, California

1991   Joyner-Kersee wins the gold medal in the long jump at the World Track and Field Championships in Tokyo, Japan

1992   At the U.S. Olympic Track and Field Trials in Indianapolis, Indiana, she wins the heptathlon; she wins gold medals in the heptathlon and long jump at the Goodwill Games; she is called "the greatest multievent athlete ever, man or woman"; given honorary Doctor of Law degree by Washington University in St. Louis, Missouri; the XXV Olympics in Barcelona, Spain, she wins her third Olympic heptathlon with 7,044 points

1993   Wins the heptathlon at the World Outdoor Track and Field
Championships in Stuttgart, Germany; Women's Sports Foundation
honors her with the McDonald's Amateur Athlete of the Year
Award

1994   Breaks her own American record in the long jump at the
USA/Mobil National Indoor Track and Field Championships in
Atlanta, Georgia; wins the 100-meter hurdles at the U.S. Olympic
Festival in St. Louis, Missouri; wins high jump and 60-meter
hurdles at the Chemical Bank Millrose Games in New York;
at the Mobil Outdoor Grand Prix Tour/Reebok New York Games,
she wins the long jump, beating her own American long-jump
record; wins the 100-meter hurdles race and long jump at the
USA-Mobil Outdoor Track and Field Championships in Knoxville,
Tennessee; at the Goodwill Games in St. Petersburg, Russia, she
wins her third straight heptathlon gold medal at this event; at the
IVO Van Damme Memorial in Brussels, Belgium, she wins the
long-jump event with a distance of 24 feet 4 inches; at the IAAF
Mobil Grand Prix Final in Paris, France, she earns the Women's
Grand Prix title with a win in the international long-jump event

INDEX

Adidas shoe company, 82
Anderson, Jodi, 70, 71
Asthma, 18–20, 57, 89, 96–97, 100, 102

Behmer, Anke, 83
Bolden, Jeanette, 80
Broderick Award, 64, 83

Cannon-Taylor, Carmen, 44, 45
Chistyakova, Galina, 91, 95
Cruz, Joaquim, 96, 97

Decathlon, 37
Didrikson, Mildred "Babe," 39–40, 84
Drechsler, Heike, 87, 95, 99

East St. Louis, Illinois, 25, 47, 52, 53, 103
800-meter run, 17, 22, 34, 53, 83, 86, 95, 101
Essence Award, 94
Evert, Sabine, 23

Fennoy, Nino, 30, 31, 32, 34, 35, 39, 41, 44
55-meter hurdles, 97
Forster, Bob, 62
400-meter hurdles, 76, 97
400-meter run, 33,
Frederick, Jane, 67, 70, 71, 73, 76, 82, 101
Freeman, Michelle, 100

Goodwill Games, 81, 83–84, 97, 101–2
Greiner, Cindy, 70, 71, 91
Griffith Joyner, Florence, 88, 91, 93, 95, 96

Heptathlon, 16–18, 20, 53, 55–57, 59, 60, 61–62, 63, 64, 67, 69–71, 76, 82, 83–84, 85, 91, 94, 95, 97, 98, 99, 101–2, 104
High jump, 17, 18, 21, 34, 70, 95, 101
Hogshead, Nancy, 57

Jackie Joyner-Kersee Community Foundation, 103, 104
Javelin throw, 17, 18, 22, 53, 55, 64, 65, 66, 67, 71, 76, 83, 86, 102
Jenner, Bruce, 100
Jesse Owens Memorial Award, 85
Johnson, Ben, 95
Johnson, Ollie Mae (great grandmother), 25, 27
Johnson, Rafer, 14
Joyner, Alfred (father), 26, 27, 31, 33, 45, 46, 53
Joyner, Alfred Erick (brother), 17, 22, 23, 27, 30, 32, 37, 45, 54, 59, 60, 61, 62, 71, 73, 79, 80, 85, 88, 89, 92, 93, 104
Joyner, Angela (sister), 26, 54, 55
Joyner, Debra (sister), 26, 54, 55
Joyner, Mary (mother), 26, 27, 31, 45, 46, 53, 54, 60, 88, 103
Joyner-Kersee, Jackie
    asthma, 18–20, 57, 89, 96–97, 100, 102
    awards and honors, 60, 64, 83, 85, 86, 94, 100

and basketball, 44, 45, 46, 47, 49–50, 57, 60, 63, 73, 74
birth, 25
childhood, 26–47, 104
education, 42, 45, 46, 50, 57, 59, 73, 74, 79, 85
and fame, 81, 82, 92, 94, 103, 104
and heptathlon, 16–18, 20, 53, 55–57, 59, 60, 61–62, 63, 64, 67, 69–71, 74, 76, 82, 83–84, 85, 91, 94, 95, 97, 98, 99, 101–2, 104
injuries, 62, 72, 95, 97, 98, 99, 102
and Junior Olympics, 30, 38–39, 41, 46, 52
and long jump, 17, 18, 21, 33–34, 45, 46, 52, 53, 55, 60, 63, 64, 65, 71, 74, 75, 83, 86, 87, 95, 98, 99, 101, 102–3
marriage, 77, 79–80
Olympic medals, 23, 72–73, 95, 99
Olympics, 16–23, 72–73, 75, 93–97, 99
Olympic trials, 46, 69–71, 91–93
and pentathlon, 34, 37, 38–39, 41, 52, 53
records set, 33, 41, 45, 46, 59, 64, 71, 74, 75, 76, 82, 83–84, 85, 86, 87, 91, 95, 97, 100, 103
7,000-point barrier, breaks, 83–84, 94
steroids, accused of using, 96–97

Junior Olympics, 30, 38–39, 41, 46, 52

Kersee, Bob (husband), 18, 21, 52, 53, 54, 55, 56, 59, 62, 63, 66, 73, 74, 75, 76, 77, 79–80, 81, 82, 83, 87, 88, 89, 97, 99, 100, 101, 103

Lincoln High School, 26, 30, 41, 42, 44, 49, 50
Long jump, 17, 18, 21, 33–34, 45, 46, 52, 53, 55, 60, 63, 64, 65, 71, 74, 75, 83, 86, 87, 91, 95, 98, 99, 101, 102–3
Louganis, Greg, 57

McDaniel, Mildred L., 95
McDonald's corporation, 104
Mary E. Brown Community Center, 27, 103
Moore, Billie, 47, 49, 50, 74, 88

National Collegiate Athletic Association (NCAA), 59, 63, 64, 76
Nunn, Glynis, 21, 22, 23

Olympic Games, 38, 61, 81
and drug testing, 19–20, 89, 95–96
history of, 13–14
1976, 37
1984, 13, 14–23, 62, 69, 72–73, 75, 88, 93, 94
1988, 85, 89, 93–97
1992, 99
1996, 104
Olympic Trials, 16, 46, 69–71, 91–93
100-meter hurdles, 17, 18, 21, 67, 70, 86, 95
Owens, Jesse, 14

Pan-American Games, 1987, 87
Pentathlon, 34, 37, 38–39, 41, 52, 53

Rudolph, Wilma, 39

7-Up soft drink company, 94
Shot put, 17, 18, 21, 34, 55, 64, 65, 66, 67, 70, 91, 95, 101
60-meter hurdles, 97, 100, 101
Steroids, 95, 96
Sullivan Award, 85

Thurston, Deborah, 49
200-meter dash, 17, 21, 82, 95, 99

University of California in Los Angeles (UCLA), 47, 50, 51, 53, 56, 59, 60, 62, 67, 73, 74, 79, 85, 86, 88, 89

Walker, Patsy, 70, 71
World Championships
1983, 61–62, 72
1987, 85, 86, 87, 88
1991, 98–99
World Class Athletic Club, 63, 82

PICTURE CREDITS

AP/Wide World Photos: pp. 17, 40, 44, 58, 62, 65, 72, 82, 87, 90, 92, 94, 95, 96, 98, 101, 102; ASUCLA Photo Department/Terry O'Donnell: pp. 47, 56, 60, 66; The Bettmann Archive: p. 14; St. Louis Mercantile Library: pp. 24, 26, 28–29, 31, 36, 48, 51, 54, 68, 71, 74, 75; Reuters/Bettmann: pp. 2, 78, 89; UPI/Bettmann: pp. 12, 22, 38, 43, 76, 84, 85, 86, 88, 93.

Geri Harrington is the author of 15 books, including *The Asthma Self-Care Book, Real Food, Fake Food and Everything in Between,* and *The Health Insurance Answer Book.* She has also written for a wide range of publications, including *Woman, Family Circle, Southern Connecticut Business Journal,* and *Grow America.* Ms. Harrington resides in Wilton, Connecticut.

Jerry Lewis is the National Chairman of the Muscular Dystrophy Association (MDA) and host of the MDA Labor Day Telethon. An internationally acclaimed comedian, Lewis began his entertainment career in New York and then performed in a comedy team with singer and actor Dean Martin from 1946 to 1956. Lewis has appeared in many films—including *The Delicate Delinquent, Rock a Bye Baby, The Bellboy, Cinderfella, The Nutty Professor, The Disorderly Orderly,* and *The King of Comedy*—and his comedy performances continue to delight audiences around the world.

John Callahan is a nationally syndicated cartoonist and the author of an illustrated autobiography, *Don't Worry, He Won't Get Far on Foot.* He has also produced three cartoon collections: *Do Not Disturb Any Further, Digesting the Child Within,* and *Do What He Says! He's Crazy!!!* He has recently been the subject of feature articles in the *New York Times Magazine,* the *Los Angeles Times Magazine,* and the *Cleveland Plain Dealer,* and has been profiled on "60 Minutes." Callahan resides in Portland, Oregon.